REDEFINE YOUR

SUCCESS

METRICS

Unveil What Success Truly Means To You And Create Your Personal Success Path

EDLYN SABRINA MCGARITY

Terms and Conditions
LEGAL NOTICE

Dedication

I dedicate this book to my parents, Solomon and Ellen, who raised me to be a strong independent-thinking woman; my children, Evangeline and Evander who gave me reasons to go on when I did not have any, and my wonderful husband, Duane for his love, care and never-ending support towards my dreams and passions.

I thank God for helping me write my first book and I pray for each one of you reading and choosing to take on this journey of redefining your Success Metrics, that this book will transform you beyond imagination.

Table of Contents

SECTION I

SECTION II

SECTION III

SECTION IV

Preface

Do you ever ask yourself, "Is there more to life?"
Whether it's your job, career, business or home, you may have given it your all, working tirelessly, sacrificing your dreams, passions, health, and relationships along the way. But you are now in your mid-life, questioning why no amount of hard work and hustle is filling the void that you feel. You are exhausted, demoralized, unfulfilled, and remorseful wondering when you stopped living and started existing. You have this lingering feeling that you were meant to accomplish more, and you have a deep desire to make a difference in the world, but you are stuck in a life that you feel you had no say in creating.

I have been there. I went through the discontentment and dissatisfaction that comes with knowing I was not being all that I was created to be.

The good news is you don't have to settle in the next season of your life. You can take back your power and create the future you desire instead of continuing on a path someone else designed for you. You can choose to rewrite your story and live an impactful, fulfilling purpose-driven life. I will share with you how my journey through trials and pains led me to a life of fulfillment and joy.

This book will help you understand how you have been influenced to live with the mediocrity mindset, assess whether your current Success Metrics are authentic to you, and create your own original success path in accordance with who you are, your values, purpose, and what you truly desire. This practical, result-driven book does not tell you what to do. Rather, it will provide a systematic guide to harness your innate power to achieve your dreams and create the life you love living. It will give you powerful strategies and tools to help you step into who you were born to be. The key to transforming your life from average to extraordinary is to reconnect with who you really are at the core.

So, join me on this journey of redefining your Success Metrics to bring true meaning, fulfillment and abundance in your life.

REDEFINE YOUR

SUCCESS

METRICS

Unveil What Success Truly Means To You And Create Your Personal Success Path

EDLYN SABRINA MCGARITY

My Success Metrics **SECTION I**

1

Introduction to Success Metrics

If I asked you, "Are you a successful person?", what would your answer be? Think about it. How do you measure success?

In this day and age, success is measured in numbers - the number of figures in our annual income, the size of our house/car/shoe collection, the number of educational credentials, our net worth, the number of followers or friends we have on the social media list, the hits/likes/clicks we get, the number of vacations we take, etc. There are metrics to measure the superlatives like most popular celebrities to follow, best brands to buy and the coolest gadgets to own.

Everything is quantified, from customer ratings to body shape and there is constant pressure to hit the highest numbers. In such a metric-driven society, the prevalent mantra is, the more the better, the higher the better, and the faster the better. But do such metrics really bring out the whole picture? Are they always synonymous with success?

In the workplace, systems and tools play a critical role in quantifying success metrics like productivity, performance, profitability, growth and customer satisfaction. As a Management Consultant, one of the common tools I used was Key Performance Indicators (KPIs). A KPI is a performance measurement that evaluates the success of an organization. However, the problem is that, like many metrics, these values do not always fully incorporate the intangibles.

However, the problem is that, like many metrics, these values do not fully incorporate the intangibles.

The KPIs cannot accurately measure elements like passion for the job, emotional health, job fulfillment, value creation, employee potential or attitude. These abstract ideas are key qualifiers for the overall success of an organization, but they may be ignored in the mix.

Whether you accept it or not, in life, you set some mental indicators that evaluate your own success and the success of others in the world. I call them the Key Life Success Indicators (KLSIs), a term I coined to use with my clients. They are like unwritten codes that influence your answer to the question I posed at the beginning of this chapter, "Are you successful?". It is possible that like KPIs, intangibles like fulfillment and meaning may be left out of your success metrics. So, a celebrity with 100,000 followers having a mean attitude may be deemed more successful by you than a social worker who serves at the homeless shelter.

> The traditional definition of success has convinced us to go wider rather than deeper, to expand outward instead of digging inward.

In the corporate world, the Key Performance Indicators (KPIs) are set in alignment with the organization's vision, mission, and objectives. Similarly, the Key Life Success Indicators (KLSIs) should typically align with your true self, your core values, and your life purpose. Unfortunately, most people set their KLSIs based on generalized success markers set by society.

We are hypnotized by society to set KLSIs for our life that measure against metrics that have been set over generations. The different factors that influence our perception of success is covered in Chapter Three.

We chase antiquated metrics without realizing that many are not relevant to this day, they are not the absolute translation of our entire state of being, and that they do not apply to everybody on the planet. The traditional definition of success has convinced us to go wider rather than deeper, to expand outward instead of digging inward. Thus, even after attaining all the wealth and fame, people end up bankrupt inside. Whatever level of success they achieve, it does not give them the ultimate satisfaction that comes from success.

Many clients tell me they want to be successful, and they want to be happy. But most often, they really do not know what that would look like to them in a way that is true to themselves. Even more tragic is the fact that, many times, people don't realize that they spend their lives pursuing KLSIs that others have set for them.

The conventional markers of success- a high paying job, a successful business, fame, being well connected, can indicate someone's outward accomplishments, but it does not cover areas pertaining to their inner reality like contentment, passion, happiness, peace, joy, meaningfulness and sense of purpose.

> True success is being able to achieve your goals and find meaning in the process. Success without fulfillment will never be satisfying.

To some, such may give them the sense of fulfillment and meaning they are seeking, but to others, such pursuits may just stroke their ego and make them feel important outwardly while bringing out the worst within them. In the process of attaining the misaligned Key Life Success Indicators (KLSIs), they lose themselves and become somebody they detest. The other such ill effects will be covered in Chapter 2. True success is being able to achieve your goals and find meaning in the process. Success without fulfilment will never be satisfying.

Everyone is unique

The fact is, KLSIs are not standard across the board. There is no one-size-fits-all measuring stick for success.

Take a moment to answer this:

If the dotted line was a measure of your success, which one would you choose?

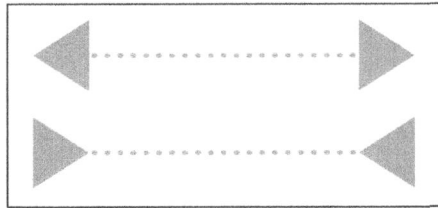

If you look closely, the lines are the same length even though one can be perceived as being longer. In the same way, success may look very different to different people since each person is unique and their internal tuning is different. We spend so much time trying to score points on someone else's Success Metric, that our personal scorecard ends up with negatives.

I remember driving outside town in Kampala, Uganda in the early years of my career and admiring the massive houses with gorgeous grassy yards and huge decks. But I would wonder why there would never be a soul sitting out there enjoying the fruits of their accomplishments. Maybe they were working late, out on business trips, or waiting to retire to enjoy their gorgeous space, I would tell myself. I secretly hoped that would not be me one day. Within me, the thought of having time to relax on such a deck was more blissful, even if the house was half the size.

My working-class mindset

Growing up in a working-class family in India, the normal life ingrained into my belief system was school, college, full-time job, marry, kids, retire. So, my Success Metrics were aligned with them. I did not know any better. We were never encouraged to think out of the box and explore other opportunities.

> But at some point, I started asking myself if that was how I wanted the rest of my life to transpire.

But at some point, I started asking myself if that was how I wanted the rest of my life to transpire; whether I wanted to work in a full-time job for more than half of my adult life. That is when, at the age of 26, I started questioning the traditional cultural attitudes towards achievement and success.

After my daughter, Evangeline was born, when I returned to work on completion of my maternity leave, I would drive home daily during lunch breaks to nurse her. I just wanted to be a mother, but I had to work, support my husband, save for investment, etc. I was immersed in the status quo- a well-paying engineering job, a full-time babysitter for my daughter, saving for investment. I was geared towards working till 65.

It broke my heart to leave my baby at home. The thought of being an independent corporate woman with a big bank account did not excite me as much as being a stay-at-home-mother, taking care of the children and home, playing with the kids, painting, and the like. Time freedom felt more in line with my Success Metric. But even if I did not need to work to support my family, leaving my well-paying, stable, prestigious job would have deemed me a failure. I am an engineer after all. With all my skills and strengths, it was a normal expectation that I would reach the peak of my engineering career. I knew I was capable of that, but deep within, that was not really what I truly desired.

4

Success means different things to different people

I started observing people and I decided to find out why some at work were so happy while others were frustrated and irritable all the time. Why some people who seemingly had nothing were joyful while others who seemingly had everything felt empty? Why did some housewives who had no job or career seem exuberant while others bitter and discontent? I learned that living a fulfilling life comes from aligning your Success Metrics with who you really are at your deepest level.

> I learned that living a fulfilling life comes from aligning your Success Metrics with who you really are at your deepest level.

You work tirelessly, struggle through the crowd, hustling, and sacrificing your family and health to climb up the ladder only to realize you were on the wrong ladder all along. That is tragic, especially if you lose yourself and what is most important to you in the process. You win the battle but lose the war.

Such misaligned Success Metrics block your mind and blind you to the endless possibilities that present themselves, leading you to a life of regret. In the pursuit of making a living, you forget to live. You dim your light. You keep trudging, pushing, chasing, and may keep getting more but it never feels enough. You begin to feel like you are chasing the wind. That results in increasing job dissatisfaction, breakdowns, stress, and burn-out.

What if you were on the wrong ladder all along? What if your KLSI was not rushing to the top of the ladder but savoring each step on the way up? What if you were supposed to stick around at a certain step to have an impact on people who would go on to change the world? What if you were not meant to climb the ladder, but to fly to the top instead?

> Such misaligned Success Metrics block your mind and blind you to the endless possibilities that present themselves.

Who sets these standards?

Who decides what is standard? Would Putlibai Gandhi and Nancy Lincoln, Mahatma Gandhi, and Abraham Lincoln's mothers respectively, qualify to be called 'successful', considering they were not independent women earning their own money? Not many knew their name, but they played a key role in shaping their son's life and

5

career. What about Hattie Mae, Oprah Winfrey's grandmother? She gave Oprah the foundation that made her the media mogul she is today. Fathers, teachers, mentors, even janitors have influenced people who have gone ahead to change the world. By the old-fashioned definition of success, they may not have news-worthy accolades to show for themselves, but I am sure they lived with the ultimate satisfaction of impacting history.

So, what if I told you that success is not what you have been taught? What if I showed you that what you believed about achievement is faulty? What if I told you that you have spent your life pursuing a lie that will only lead to disappointment?

There is no one 'best way' or one standard path to success. I have met joyful vegetable vendors, passionate house-helps and I have met troubled multimillionaires and exasperated entrepreneurs. I have seen sad, troubled, and unfulfilled people regardless of their bank balance, occupation, status, fame, and looks. I have spoken to spiritual leaders, stay-at home-mothers, entrepreneurs, and volunteers who were equally anxious, hopeless, and burned-out. There is no one 'best way' or one standard path to success. Quitting your job, time freedom, renouncing all possessions, and even going on a pilgrimage will not guarantee fulfillment. Each person is unique and so is their Success Metric.

No right or wrong KLSI
There is no right or wrong KLSI. It is what is right or wrong for you. In Chapter Four, I will share some guidelines that will help you assess whether your Success Metrics is aligned with your true self. To someone, having a thriving business is a measure of success, to another being a doctor and yet to another, it may mean being a comedian, a writer, sportsperson, or a technician.

My mother worked as a teacher for about 50 years. She had no problem reporting to a boss, neither did she mind the structured lifestyle. For most of her career, she did not do it for the money or the status. Teaching was her passion and brought out the best in her. Her delight was seeing her students each day and having a positive impact on their lives. Working in a full-time job till she was seventy was success for her. Personally, I would not trade places with a business mogul who is obligated to work 40 hours a week, even if I was offered millions of Dollars. But time freedom and work flexibility may not be everyone's Success Metric.

Being aware of what success means to you and pursuing it instead of blindly following others' KLSIs will positively impact your quality of life and state of mind. The way you define success for yourself has a huge impact on your choices, work, responses, and how you create your life.

"To live is the rarest thing in the world. Most people exist, that is all." Oscar Wilde

Your Success Metric may seem irrational to others
When I met my husband, Duane, he was working in an extremely stressful job in Air Traffic Control. One of the things that drew me to him was his plan to retire before the age of fifty. To me, a successful relationship is based on spending quality time together, something that eluded me in my first marriage.

When Duane was nearing fifty, we revisited the two options he had: continuing to work and earn substantially more money or taking early retirement. His job came with intense pressure, where one mistake could result in the loss of several hundred lives. That was a reason why Air Traffic Controllers were having one of the highest divorce and suicide rates of any career field in the US. So, we made a decision to choose early retirement, which helped him retire in good health and also gave him time freedom, both of which were more important to us.
Unfortunately, several of his colleagues who chose to work beyond their early retirement eligibility date died before retiring or shortly after retiring due to heart attacks and other stress-related illnesses.

What success means to you may seem illogical to others, but the key is raising your level of self-awareness, defining what success means to you in line with your design and purpose, and confidently pursuing it. It may not always conform to the standards of others and will take courage to break the cycle, but when you start following your success path, each moment of the day will come alive with wonder. On the other hand, you may be exactly where you are supposed to be, but don't realize it because you are measuring your life with others' yardsticks of success.

Your life is your responsibility.

Setting KLSIs that ensures joy and fulfillment in your life is your responsibility. It is up to you to find your best path to success, run your race and finish strong. You can choose to continue living life in on autopilot clinging to a false sense of significance and security, letting someone else dictate your experience, or you can choose to design the life that is true to you. You cannot do both.

It is up to you to find your best path to success, run your race and finish strong. Redefining success at work will help you find meaning in your career. Redefining success in your marriage, friendships, and associations will help you enjoy authentic relationships. Redefining success in your finances will help you feel contentment as you continue to aspire for more.

What is covered in the rest of the book?

There is no formula for a successful life, but this book will help you choose the right KLSIs for yourself by helping you discard your old ideas about achievement and take action towards your renewed definition of success. That way, you can stop existing and start living and experience deep fulfillment, satisfaction, passion, and success in what you do every day.

In the rest of SECTION I, I will help you to understand the importance of setting the right KLSIs and the reasons we subconsciously adhere to faulty Success metrics. Chapter Four will help to evaluate your current KLSIs and assess if there are any vital areas you have neglected.

SECTION II of this book will help you to break free of beliefs that hold you back, gain an understanding of your true identity and value system, and to uncover your purpose and true desires.

Building on what you uncover, SECTION III of this book will help you to extract your personal KLSIs that will allow you to step into who you were born to be, and set goals and action steps to achieve a life of fulfillment, abundance, and joy.

There are worksheets at the end of each chapter to use for the exercises in the book. If you want to download all the worksheets in one place, you can use this link:

DOWNLOAD WORKSHEETS

To access FREE printable versions of the worksheets in one place:
https://www.edlynsabrina.com/successmetricstoolkit

Conclusion

I resigned from my full-time job in 2004 when my son, Evander was born and have been working on my terms since then. I was able to be present for my kids during the weekends and school breaks. That is success to me.

A few years back my parents visited us in Ohio for 4 months. I was able to spend each day with them without worrying about a boss, deadlines, meetings, or business trips. That is success to me.

I can wake up each morning and decide how I want the day to go. That is success to me.

I receive messages every other day from people who say how I have inspired them to change their lives. That is success to me.

Setting your personal Success Metric and living in alignment with it, will give you joy in your daily pursuits, empower you to expand your potential, and live your best version unapologetically.

Make a pact with yourself today not to be defined by other people's measure of success. Instead, take back your power and design your version of success with intentionality. You will be doing a favor for yourself and the world around you.

Setting your personal Success Metric and living in alignment with it, will give you joy in your daily pursuits and empower you to expand your potential and live your best version unapologetically. Redefining success in line with your true identity, values, strengths, and higher purpose, creating your unique best success path, and walking on it will lead you to true fulfillment.

ACTIVITY

Write down the Key Life Success Indicators on your scoreboard at this time:

Now, be honest with yourself and ask these questions:
- Who has set it for you? Are these really your KLSIs?
- Do you have old measures of success that you need to redefine?
- Does it cover what is most important to you? Will these bring true happiness and fulfillment to you?
- Are you fixated on only external definitions of success?

NOTES

2

The Gravity of the problem

The seemingly perfect career path

When I started my career as a computer engineer, I knew I was on the right path. I had worked hard to earn an engineering degree. My dream, like that of 90% of the workforce, was to work hard, reach the highest career point possible and eventually work in the best corporation in my industry.

I completed my Microsoft Certified System Engineer Certifications, while I was nursing my little daughter and working full-time. I traveled to Nairobi and the US for conferences, trainings and was taking on more job responsibilities. I was on a roll and well on my way to reaching my dreams. With the support from my parents, I was able to invest in real estate and we had started building rental units on it. My Key Life Success Indicators

> That was a dream ingrained into my subconscious through my upbringing based on cultural attitudes towards achievement.

(KLSIs) included a lucrative career, owning a commercial building and growing a commercial eucalyptus and pine tree forest. My dream mostly revolved around creating financial wealth and I was heading there.

But five years into that career, I realized that that was not my true dream. That was a dream ingrained into my subconscious through my upbringing based on cultural attitudes towards achievement. They were well-meaning, profitable KLSIs, but they were not what I genuinely wanted. I was good at my job and my performance was good, but within me, I knew I was out of alignment in some way. And as I started questioning my beliefs and questioning the norm, I began to realize that I did not even know myself, what exactly I wanted, and what truly made me happy. I was working towards the society's KLSIs.

That deep quest for more left me never feeling fully satisfied with my performance and success. I dreaded Mondays and looked forward

11

to staying at home with my growing daughter. Even when I was at home sick, I felt happier. I explored creative opportunities at work, even went on field trips and I loved doing that, but I was not thriving. On the outside, I had the perfect job, but I knew I was not maximizing my potential and was untrue to my true design. My ex-husband did not understand why I felt uninspired and that strained our relationship. So, I continued in the rat race, supressing the real me and trudging my way through life, giving it my all.

In any case, even if I wanted to quit my job and be a stay-at-home mother, I did not have any option, or so I thought. I needed those "golden handcuffs" to pay for the home expenses. My husband and I were just 5 years into our career, and we needed the money. I was stuck there because I couldn't afford to leave, financially. I had this limiting belief that there was no other way.

Whose dream are you chasing?

I believed that was part of life. I appreciate that one cannot achieve any significant success without putting in efforts and energy. I also was aware that many times, achieving your big dreams can entail a lot of sacrifices. I was wholeheartedly willing to pay the price to reach those dreams. But I was not sure those were my dreams I was chasing. And that is happening with a lot of the people in the world. You are not aware of your authentic self and true desires and end up chasing others' dreams without realizing it. On the other hand, you may know what you want, but you feel stuck in the status quo because of the fear of the unknown, fear of being judged, the lack of confidence, or the deception that things will get better by itself.

You are not aware of your authentic self and true desires and end up chasing others' dreams without realizing it.

Coping with inner conflict

To compensate for the inner conflict, and in the quest of feeling happier or more accomplished, you drown yourself in work, trying to hit the highest targets, get the highest promotions and endless home projects. You reach your goals and before the dust settles you start looking for the next target. You use work, projects, partying, social work, drugs, binge-watching TV, alcohol, shopping, and the like as distractions to avoid confronting reality. You keep moving from one emotional high to another, but still feel empty.

Chasing after others' dreams can work for some time and I did that. I pretended everything was good and was determined to go on that way for the rest of my life. But living out of alignment with your truest self will take a toll at a deeper level, gnawing at you and chipping away at your self-worth and your passion and will to live.

"There is no agony like bearing an untold story inside you" Maya Angelou

Things don't just fall into place

The other agony I was enduring of being untrue to myself, was my marriage. It was a painful and emotionally abusive experience, but I was clinging to it because that was the normal thing to do. I was not allowed to be myself, make friends, follow my passions, or authentically express myself in the marriage. I was willing to continue that way in the marriage forever, pretending to be someone I was not. Even when things got worse when I resigned from my job to take care of my two-month-old baby boy, I convinced myself that things would fall into alignment on their own. They don't.

If you want to align your life with who you truly are, you need to take action towards it. If not, as you keep getting away from your path, you end up getting drained, irritable, bored and fatigued even with simple tasks. Such discontent and dissatisfaction lead to depression, anxiety, and stress-related health issues.

But living out of alignment with your truest self will take a toll at a deeper level, gnawing at you and chipping away at your self-worth and your passion and will to live.

The result of misalignment

The frustration at work, home, business, or your relationships overflows beyond that space and you end up projecting the exhaustion and bitterness onto the very people you live for, the ones you are striving for in the first place. You disconnect with those closest to you, which results in resentment and more bitterness. Some keep pushing on with that unhealthy balance in their attitude towards success even when their life falls apart.

The hopelessness of being stuck, not willing to get out, or not aware of how to, amplifies the inner conflict that will continue till it explodes in the worst way resulting in even psychological and physical collapse. Towards the end of my dysfunctional marriage, I faced all that and was just one step away from a total breakdown. Even if the

13

consequences are not that drastic and you feel you are doing a good job at surviving, you will fail to thrive. Your growth will be stifled and will not flourish, and you know it within you.

The obvious solution may not be right for you
The logical solution may seem like getting out of the situation, renouncing material possessions, taking on a new venture or religion. But those will leave you even more purposeless, exasperated and hollow if it does not align with your true design.

'Be your own boss' and 'time freedom' may be the Success Metrics for some people, for others, it may be "working till you retire", "start a non-profit organization" or "being a stay-at-home mom". I have seen stay-at-home mothers, entrepreneurs, spiritual leaders, corporate professionals equally burned out. I have also seen retirement and entrepreneurship bring out the worst in people.

You dim your light
When you are not true to yourselves, you eventually burn out and become somebody you do not recognize. You dim your light, which was meant not just for you, but for making a difference in the world.

> When you are not true to yourselves, you eventually burn out and become somebody you do not recognize.

Each person is unique and has a unique combination of talents, gifts, personality, passion, and experience, and each person is called for a unique purpose. Uncovering my purpose was an interesting journey for me, a journey that I enjoyed and flourished in. 16 years after resigning from my full-time job, searching for answers through my passions, social work, and expression of art, I learned that the answer lied within. I just needed to pay attention.

Whether you believe it or not, you are called for greatness. You have a role to play in the world in your unique way. And deep inside, you know that living outside your purpose is causing a deficit in somebody else's life. And the knowledge that you are not living your life of significance will gnaw at you. Instead of focusing on identifying your calling and pursuing it, you work extremely hard trying to do the seemingly right or acceptable thing, looking for answers in all outward directions.

Getting tossed in the wind

Without clarity of what you want and where you want to go, you get tossed in different directions, seduced by shallow offers to make your life better. You end up accumulating things you never wanted, doing things to please others, and being someone you do not even like. You get sucked up by the latest fads, the most lucrative opportunities, the fanciest brands and nothing is ever enough. These vain exploits in all random directions take you away from what you are built for and your truest dreams.

"We buy things we don't need with money we don't have to impress people we don't like." Either Dave Ramsey or Will Smith.

The result of living in alignment

Your journey towards living life by design instead of default mode may not be smooth sailing. It will call for efforts, perseverance and sacrifice, and the destination may not be without storms, but it will be worth it. You will wake up each day excited about this intentional journey towards building and living a life that is in alignment with your true self and your purpose and abundance will flow in ways you cannot imagine. You will feel alive, passionate, and lit up from within, knowing you are being what you were born to be and are making a difference in the world in your unique way.

ACTIVITY

Are you experiencing any ill-effects of living a life disconnected from your true self and pursuing culturally fabricated Success Metrics? Circle all that apply.

LACK OF CONFIDENCE   BITTERNESS   REMORSE   BURN-OUT   IRRITABILITY
FATIGUE   EXHAUSTION   DISCONTENT   RESENTMENT   DISSATISFACTION
ANXIETY   CHRONIC STRESS   BOREDOM   FRUSTRATION   PSYCHOLOGICAL
EFFECTS   MENTAL HEALTH DISORDERS   INNER CONFLICT   SNAPPING WITH
FAMILY EMOTIONAL OUTBURSTS   NO SENSE OF PURPOSE   SLEEP DISORDERS
STAGNATION   NERVOUS BREAKDOWNS   EMPTINESS   LOSS OF MEANING

Any other ill-effects?

Give this some thought:
Are you building a life you are proud of? Do you wake up each day excited about it?

NOTES

3

The Origins of The Problem

Human psychology

As humans, we are hardwired to seek approval and conform to social norms. We pick up social cues on good, bad, right, wrong, normal, and acceptable and build our beliefs around them. We align our behavior, goals, and plans around those generalized metrics.

Such metrics have helped in survival and building civilizations and resulted in great progress and development in society. But there is evidence throughout history that such conformity to social cues, whether normative or informative has unfavorable results. We have seen how entire marginalized groups have been wiped out through genocides because of people who did not dare to question or refuse their order. So, regardless of whether the decision leads to painful, miserable consequences or goes against our values, conformity soothes.

Recent research has shown that social disapproval provokes the brain's dangerous circuits.

More often than not, we are not aware that we are conforming. We believe things to be normal that are not normal for the masses. So, when you think or talk about success, as per your brain wiring, you have already picked up acceptable Key Life Success Indicators (KLSIs) from your social influences.

Limiting beliefs and cultural norms

During the time of our ancestors, the Success Metrics probably were generalized to survival - protecting their family and having food and shelter. The fastest way to hunt, the number of days you have food stored for and how long you live could have been part of the general KLSIs for the masses. And we continue to live today believing that everyone can find fulfilment following standard paths.

When you look at Maslow's hierarchy of needs, the lower levels are considered the deficit mode. But the definition of deficit has changed radically in these modern days. The basic need of food, shelter and safety is still non-negotiable across the board, but we can no longer generalize what someone's intrinsic need is and what will fill that gap. We find people who have gone up all levels of the hierarchy and are still empty and seeking more. That could be why Maslow had begun to have doubts about his model toward the end of his life.

Human beings have evolved, the entire work dynamics have revolutionized, and the ancient ideologies are irrelevant in the present time.

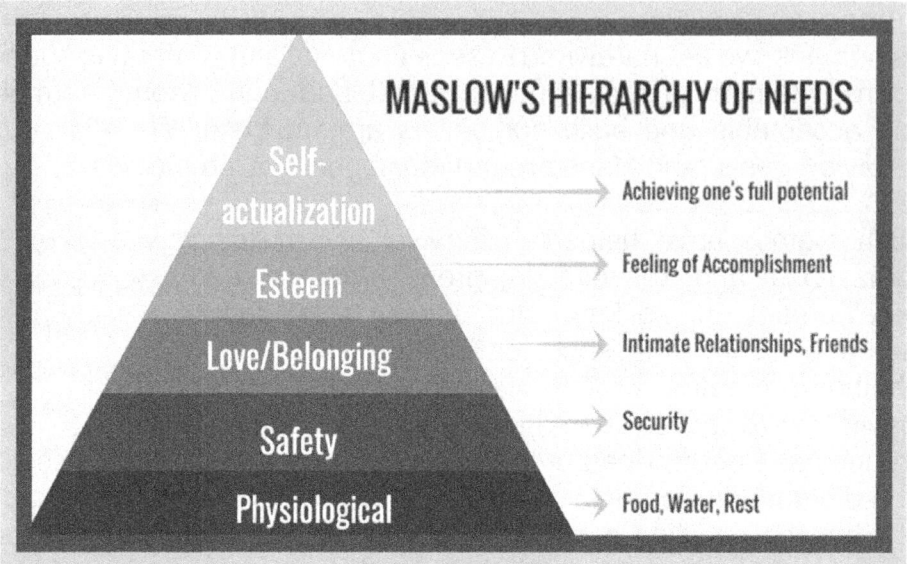

MASLOW'S HIERARCHY OF NEEDS

Self-actualization → Achieving one's full potential

Esteem → Feeling of Accomplishment

Love/Belonging → Intimate Relationships, Friends

Safety → Security

Physiological → Food, Water, Rest

It's not just hunters and gatherers now, we have doctors, actors, firemen, comedians, fashion designers, telemarketers, homemakers, and professors. Each one has a unique design, unique talent, and a unique calling that makes them happy.

But we continue to rely on unrealistic, generalized legacy Success Metrics that are ingrained into our subconscious mind right from our childhood. They are our default mode. Nobody questions them and they continue to exist. These metrics drive us to burn-out, job dissatisfaction, anxiety, emptiness and depression

Examples of flawed Success Metrics

One example is the way test scores of a child in school supposedly imply the child's intelligence and IQ. Most examinations do not assess the knowledge of the student or his ability to process the learning to explore new possibilities. Rather, they assess what the student can memorize and can successfully reproduce on the day of the examination. So, a child may grow up to think he is dumb, and to confine himself within the box. He learns more about what he is

bad at, rather than what he could be good at. There is no test to assess what the child was created to be and how he can someday explore a hidden capability to make a difference in the world.
My husband was told by his teacher he would not amount to anything, but he went on to build a successful career with the

Einstein said, "Everybody is a genius. But if you judge a fish by its ability to climb a tree, it will live its whole life believing that it is stupid"

federal government and is one of the few people in the world who has been able to retire, financially free, before the age of 50.

Conventional wisdom teaches us 'the best way', 'the fastest way', 'the only way to success'. Unfortunately, these are based on principles that are becoming more and more irrelevant over time. But they are ingrained into our subconscious mind as normal and we accept it and pursue it without questioning, instead of trying to create your own best path to success.

The traditional view is that your less than spectacular high school grades would lead to higher chances of failure. But if that was a standard measure of success, then the top brass of society would consist of solely valedictorians and not people like Bill Gates, Richard Branson and Steve Jobs who were all college dropouts

Money is considered the measure of success. The more you have, the more you are considered successful. If that was true, every wealthy person in the world would be happy. Many wealthy people are very happy and lead meaningful life, but there are others to whom 'more' is never enough. One example is the studies that show that most lottery winners end up depressed or committing suicide.

Fame is another traditional marker of success, but is it really? How would you explain depression, breakdowns and suicides among celebrities? Some know how to manage fame and keep themselves grounded; others just lose themselves under the glory and pressure of the limelight.

Conventional wisdom is settling for a well-paying job, regardless of whether it gives you satisfaction and meaning, or whether you excel at it; accumulating as much as you can, retiring when you can no longer work, and then living your dreams, if still possible, for the remaining years of your life. So, you achieve the height of success according to the generalized Success Metric but are not satisfied. You still feel empty and lose meaning in your life, because you are not living your true design in line with your higher purpose. Instead of taking the time to discover the gifts you were born with and maximizing them, you give away control of your future.

You may be clinging to the status quo for fear of being judged, but it's you who is accountable for your joy and fulfillment.

So, what if all the success markers we have learned to accept are wrong? What if it does not apply to everybody on the globe. What if you have a unique purpose and a unique path that will take you to your unique success metric.

"Settling" and adapting to the job, career path, relationship and mental space that does not bring your satisfaction or suppresses your true potential can work short-term, but in the long-term, it will cause more harm than good, regardless of your intentions and motivations.

You may have a subconscious belief that achieving success and living a life of meaning are two different paths. But that is not true You are a multi-dimensional human being and squeezing yourself into one box that is smaller than you can be detrimental.

You may confine yourself to the general KLSIs to keep up with the Joneses, but you will never be successful because their journey is different. You may be clinging to the status quo for fear of being judged, but it's you who is accountable for your joy and fulfillment. What people say many times is a projection of their own limiting beliefs and narrow-minded perspectives.

If Walt Disney gave in to what people talked about him when he was rejected everywhere, we would have been deprived of world-class entertainment. If Thomas Edison gave in, considering he had failed 10,000 times, we would have missed his contribution to the invention of the light bulb, phonograph and motion picture camera. If Martin Luther King Jr. had succumbed to what people said, the people and generations that followed would have been deprived of the tremendous inspiration he offered.

Comfort zone

Your fear of failure, uncertainty, or being criticized makes you snuggle deeper into your comfort zone, to the extent that even the pain and frustration comforts you. You eventually choose the familiarity of your misery over the joy of living in liberty of your fullest self and that is tragic. There is no 'One way to Success' or standard KLSIs and it takes courage to fight the norm.

> You eventually choose the familiarity of your misery over the joy of living in liberty of your fullest self and that is tragic.

The world is full of people who refused to follow the default mode and created their own destiny. They formulated their personal definition of success and live fulfilling and meaningful lives playing their part in leaving this world a better place.

ACTIVITY

What are the "You should..." and "You are supposed to...." statements that you have been passed on to you that you are adhering to right now?

What are some of the statements above that do not make sense to you on a deeper level? What statements do not feel true to you?

Which areas of your life would you like to see a change in relation to the above?

NOTES

4

Assessment

So, are you living your personal Key Life Success Indicators (KLSIs), or are you consciously or unconsciously living your life endeavoring to measure up to someone else's KLSIs?

Whether we admit it or not, the traditional definition of success always involves money, material acquisitions, and fame. We perceive a high-profile actor owning a jet as successful even if he is arrogant or on the verge of a drug overdose. A housewife who is the happiest raising her kids and joyfully nurturing them may not be perceived as successful by most people.

The purpose of this chapter is to help you evaluate whether your Key Life Success Indicators are true to you, by helping you become aware of your past influences, present circumstances, and probable trajectories.

> The awareness will enable you to take back your power to create happiness and joy right where you are.

There is a popular saying, "If it ain't broke, don't fix it." Unfortunately, we live only once and it may be too late to fix things like relationships and health, once it is broken. If you see a strain, a crack, or tear, working on it sooner may prevent irreversible damage. Examining your KLSIs will help you assess if you are in a place that does not bring out the best in you and assess the gaps between what you think you want and what you truly want.

At the end of the assessment, you may discover that you are already living your Success Metrics. You may not have realized it because they look very different than the world's view of success. So, you keep going on in deficit mode without appreciating the wonders of your abundant life. Being aware that your KLSIs is authentic to you, will help you see that your life does not really need fixing. It will help you celebrate all you have achieved and smile in your heart each new day. The awareness will enable you to take back your power to create happiness and joy right where you are.

Silencing the noise so you can listen to yourself

As we learned in the previous chapter, your deep-rooted belief systems influence the way you live your life and how, most times, you are not even aware that those beliefs limit you from being who you are, sometimes it even goes against what you stand for.

In the middle of the pandemic in 2020, my mother called me from Mumbai to tell me how the birds had got louder. And then it hit me, that it was not the birds that had gotten louder, the noise had quieted down. Mumbai is one of the noisiest cities in the world and because of the COVID pandemic, the city that never sleeps, suddenly shut down. Thus, with all the silence, the birds sounded louder.

> You don't consider looking back to assess all you have lost and whether those were worth losing.

As you go through life, you get so caught up with your routine, to-do lists, work, home, family and social events that your inner voice gets silenced. To add to that, life gets so noisy with all the seductive distractions of the world, that you lose direction of where you are going. You keep working to the bone, hustling and rushing without pausing to check around you to ascertain whether you are on the right path. You don't consider looking back to assess all you have lost and whether those were worth losing.

You get so busy being busy that you stop hearing your inner voice and your intuition. While constantly reaching for more, you take for granted the life that has been given to you. You may attain the wealth and the fame you so desperately seek, but soon recognize how bankrupt you still remain.

You may be living your life comparing your accomplishments, occupation, possessions, job titles, body, even kids with other people. And nothing seems enough because there is always somebody with a better career, a bigger house, a better body, more money and more expensive cars.

The exercises in this chapter will help quieten the noise around and raise your awareness of yourself, your current environment, and your life balance to evaluate if you are living a life true to your KLSIs.

Don't Settle

I came across this illustration on the Internet which has a powerful message. I do not know the accuracy of the statistics in the illustration, but from my experience, it is not very far from the truth.

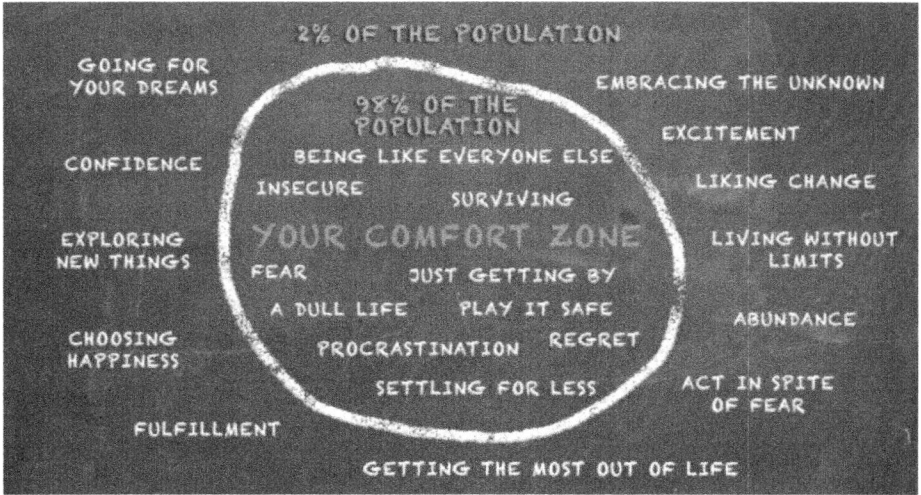

2% OF THE POPULATION

GOING FOR YOUR DREAMS

EMBRACING THE UNKNOWN

98% OF THE POPULATION

EXCITEMENT

CONFIDENCE

BEING LIKE EVERYONE ELSE

INSECURE

SURVIVING

LIKING CHANGE

YOUR COMFORT ZONE

EXPLORING NEW THINGS

FEAR

JUST GETTING BY

LIVING WITHOUT LIMITS

A DULL LIFE   PLAY IT SAFE

CHOOSING HAPPINESS

PROCRASTINATION   REGRET

ABUNDANCE

SETTLING FOR LESS

ACT IN SPITE OF FEAR

FULFILLMENT

GETTING THE MOST OUT OF LIFE

Observing this, I would say about 2% of the people live their life according to their personal Success Metrics. The other 98 % are either not aware that they are off-track or are too scared to get down from the wrong ladder and climb up the right one.

Their fear of failure or being judged is greater than the excitement of walking in their personal Success Path. So, they settle for far less than they deserve or are capable of and they live their life full of regret, brooding over opportunities they missed and over what could have been.

Their fear of failure or being judged is greater than the excitement of walking in their personal Success Path.

Whatever situation you are in, if you are reading this book, you want more out of your life. Either you seek more depth and meaning in your life and want to figure out how to get from where you are to where you want to be. On the other hand, you may want to understand why despite having everything you need and want, you feel it's not enough. You may be someone who has tried everything by the book, following the societal norms to the dot, without seeing results. You are seeking the missing part of the puzzle.
Am I on the right ladder?

When I am asked "How will I know I am on the right ladder?", the simplest one-line answer I give is "The results will show". If a tree is growing healthily, it will bear fruits, delicious fruits, fruits that are pleasing to the sight, taste and experience of those around. Some trees need more watering, others need more sun. Similarly, what works for one may not work for another, but the results won't lie.

And the answer lies within you. If you pay attention and pick up the cues, you will be able to notice. Don't worry if you feel there is a high wall between where you think you are and where you are. Just be honest with yourself as you take these tests that will help you assess whether you are on the right track. Ponder the questions in each section for a few minutes, focusing on only one question at a time.

TEST 1. The Potential Test

Are you convinced that you are maximizing your potential to the fullest where you are right now? Do you feel your knowledge, personality, natural talents, skills, passions, personality, competence, and resourcefulness are utilized to the maximum?

Working as an Engineer, I realized that I was not optimizing my potential. I was good at my job, the profession was good, the pay was quite competitive, and the environment was healthy. But there was something inside me struggling to come out and I did not know what it was. When training was added to my job description, I remember not being excited about it at first. I had never taught before, doubted I could do it and I did not enjoy the thought of training. But when I started doing it, I enjoyed it. I got great feedback about my training style and delivery and how I could simplify a complex topic. And that is how I discovered my skills in training, even though it was a small part of my job. Soon I realized that working as an engineer, surrounded by computers and servers for most of my day, was not what I wanted to do for the rest of my life.

Years later, as I started exploring my potential, I discovered my love for working with people, painting, entrepreneurship, art, acting, writing, and the like. In my job, I was exercising my systematic, logical left brain, but my equally dominant creative right brain was stagnating. I felt my skills were grossly underutilized. So, I expanded my capacity by getting an MBA and started doing freelance management consultancy jobs while pursuing speaking and acting. I am now at the point in my life where I wake up excited each day knowing that I won't take my gifts to the grave.

Are you utilizing your potential?

Research shows that 45% of Americans in the workforce did not feel they were utilizing their full potential and from talking to people in different parts of the world, I feel that statistic may be applicable across the globe. Research has shown that many people are not even aware of their strengths. If you are in a place where your secondary capabilities are used more than your strengths, you may be heading towards frustration, disappointment and feelings of inadequacy. You will be more productive and can accomplish more if you were in a place where you can hone your strengths and utilize your fullest potential.

Further, research has shown that not living in line with your strengths will result in a state of unhappiness, because your strengths are the essence of who you are at your core, and utilizing your strengths will allow you to be your best self, thus resulting in higher levels of well-being.

> If you are in a place where your secondary capabilities are used more than your strengths, you may be heading towards frustration, disappointment and feelings of inadequacy.

Questions for Introspection:

Are you aware of your strengths?
Are you required to do a lot of tasks that you do not have a natural bent for?
Do the tasks you do come easy to you?
Do you feel you are utilizing most of your strengths?
Does your work allow you to build your strengths while paying less attention to your weakness?
Are these activities in any way related to your hobbies, interests?
Do you feel authentic to yourself?

If you answered No to most of these questions, your Key Life Success Indicators are not in sync with who you truly are. Discovering, developing, and maximizing your potential will bring fulfillment and inspiration to life and you should consider that when setting your KLSI.

27

TEST 2. Growth Test

Everything in nature is in motion, it is either growing or decaying. So, what is happening to you? Look at your life exactly five years back on this date and ask yourself these questions

Questions for Introspection:
Do you think you have grown?
Have you acquired new skills and knowledge?
Are your strengths being continually developed?
Can you do more now than you could five years back?
Have you accomplished more?
Are you a better person? Are you a better parent, partner, citizen?

If you have more 'No's, you are not growing and thriving and that indicates that your Key Life Success Indicators are not authentic to you. If you perceive yourself as not having changed that is equally bad, because the truth is nothing stays stagnant. Either there is improvement or degradation. Whatever space you are in, whether in your relationship, job, home, business, or personal life, if you are unable to improve and flourish for long periods, your life will ultimately lead to dissatisfaction and discouragement, regardless of performance.

Please be aware that if your environment is causing you to degenerate, then without a doubt, it is a toxic space for you. You need to step back, look at the fuller picture and make a decision to move on.

Additionally, remember that as you keep growing, you may need to clear spaces to expand or move to spaces where you can spread yourself. Sometimes we try to squeeze ourselves into a box that we have outgrown and that can be demotivating, painful and demoralizing.

TEST 3: Fulfilment Test

It would be valuable if there was a device to gauge fulfillment. That would enable many people to make choices to get back on track sooner. Unfortunately, your fulfillment is something only you can assess, and you have to be honest with yourself about it. What brings you fulfillment may not mean anything to another person.

In my quest for fulfillment, I pursued several passions post my engineering career and I have several successes under my belt. I won the Mrs. India Uganda title, I landed lead and supporting roles in feature films, my paintings were displayed in galleries and I have appeared on a magazine cover and even a national billboard. However, I came to learn that fame, accomplishments and accolades do not always directly correlate to fulfillment.

> However, I came to learn that fame, accomplishments and accolades do not always directly correlate to fulfillment.

There are three areas I want to cover under fulfilment- happiness, peace, and chronic stress.

Happiness/Joy
Happiness is misinterpreted as most people focus on the emotional aspect of happiness. But ask yourself, are you really content? Are you constantly irritated doing what you are doing? Are you feeling burned out? Are you excited about the opportunities you have each day to be the best you can be? Professionals, minimum wage workers, housewives, entrepreneurs, social workers, all alike may feel sadness or frustration. So, having a prestigious career, money, fame, or lack thereof is not a predictor of joy. True happiness comes from a joy that soars from within, regardless of external circumstances.

Peace
Another test of fulfillment is having peace amidst the storm. Fulfillment does not come from a perfect life, without any challenge, but it comes from knowing with utmost certainty that you are where you are meant to be. You will experience an unexplainable inner peace when you are living in alignment. And that peace will confirm that you are being true to yourself.

Chronic Stress
A marker that shows a lack of fulfillment is the stress accompanied by your role. A certain amount of stress is normal and even helpful.

But if you are constantly in a state of stress, to the extent that it affects you physically and physiologically, you are definitely in the wrong place. When you walk in the path meant for you, you will feel in the flow and live in abundance.

But if you are constantly in a state of stress, to the extent that it affects you physically and physiologically, you are definitely in the wrong place.

Questions for Introspection:
Are you feeling the joy within?
Do you derive happiness from what you do?
Are you feeling energized and complete?
Do you enjoy what you are doing?
Are you at peace with how your life is right now?
Do you feel you are true to yourself in the place you are right now?
Do you feel you are headed in the right direction?
Do you feel that what you are doing is aligning with your values?
Are you feeling deeply satisfied and passionate about what you do?
Are your stress levels at reasonable levels most times?
If you answered No to most of these questions, you are most likely not living in the KLSIs that are healthy for you and you are diminishing your chances for a joyful and fulfilling life.

TEST 4: Performance Test
If you are in a place that is right for you, you will be thriving in terms of the quality of your work. You will no doubt excel when you are in the right place, because you were not created for mediocrity.

"The heart of human excellence often begins to beat when you discover a pursuit that absorbs you, frees you, challenges you, or gives you a sense of meaning, joy, or passion." Terry Orlick

You will be pleased with your performance without feeling the need to validate it by comparing it with that of others. Your efforts and hard work in that area will bear exponential results.

Questions for Introspection:
Do you feel that you are great at what you do?
Are you satisfied with your work and how well you do it?
Do people come to you for advice/ support in what you are doing?

Do you utilize your strengths to achieve excellent results?
Do you get great results easily?
If you answered No to most of these, it's time you take a second look and re-evaluate your situation. If you have been in a place for a long time and your performance is not satisfactory to you, you may be climbing up the wrong ladder towards success.

It is very important to remember that you may be misaligned with your true self and still perform well because of your resilience and dedication. My performance was exceptional as an engineer, though that was not my true Success Path. But when you are in alignment, there is no doubt that you will perform exceptionally.

TEST 5. Balance Test

I read an article where Rishi Kapoor, a beloved Bollywood icon who died of cancer recently, was said to have quoted this a few years before his death, "I never made friends with Ranbir (his only son) and it's a deep regret". That is indeed unfortunate. In the last chapter of our life's journey, it would be sad to have such regrets. As you toil day in and day out, pursuing success, wealth, and fame, don't forget what is most important to you. Health, wealth, and relationships are non-negotiables when it comes to KLSIs. If your success journey is neglecting any of these, you are headed towards disappointment.

> As you toil day in and day out, pursuing success, wealth, and fame, don't forget what is most important to you.

Do not lose sight or neglect the people who matter the most. You may say that you are working and sacrificing for the sake of your children, but ironically, you do it at the cost of your relationship with them. Your incongruent lifestyle leaves you so drained that you lash out at your children and spouse. It is not just those working in 9-5 jobs that are guilty of such imbalance. Interestingly, I have met church workers and volunteers who are so busy saving the world that they neglect or lose theirs.

You may be working to the bone to reach your goals and, in the process, you ignore the red flags and end up with several health problems, some of which can be life-threatening. On the other hand, you may be busy following your passions and end up not having money to pay the bills or end up becoming a burden to others.

Alternately, you may have reached the pinnacle of success, but lose your soul and end up despising who you have become. Such imbalance calls for a reassessment of your KLSIs.

"What will it benefit a person if he gains the whole world and loses his own soul" The Bible.

You are a multidimensional human being, playing multiple roles. And there is a need, now more than ever, for you to balance your life to live a happy, fulfilling life. The questions below can help assess your life balance.

Questions for Introspection:
Do you recognize who you really are?
Are you happy with who you have become?
Are you taking time to nurture your close relationships?
Are you taking time for self-care and self-love?
Are you taking time to rest, have fun and unwind?
Are you happy with the state of your health and where it is heading?
If you have more No's, your life is out of balance there is a need for you to make some drastic changes in your KLSIs. When you put all of your energy into one thing and neglect the others, you cannot maintain a healthy balance.

QUICK TIP
There is a Wheel of life exercise on Page 137 that can help you further assess your Life Balance.

TEST 6. Impact Test
Do your Key Life Success Indicators make life better for someone other than yourself? Living a successful life is not just about what you are doing for yourself and your family, but the impact you have beyond them. You don't have to switch career paths to be a doctor or firefighters to save lives. You can directly or indirectly impact lives right where you are. The impact you create may be seen immediately or may be felt long after you are gone. But the truth is we were not created to just serve ourselves.

You may impact your company with your creativity or through mentoring your team member. You may be a housewife supporting your husband behind the scene to have the impact. You may be the comedian who brings laughter or a retiree who volunteers. You may be a stay-at-home mother raising your child with the right values to grow up to be someone who changes the world.

Zig Ziglar said, "You can have everything in life you want if you just help enough other people get what they want!"

Regardless of how you define your Success Metrics, if it does not suggest your contribution to the bigger picture and make a difference in others' lives, then you may be on the wrong track.

Questions for Introspection:
Do you engage in activities that benefit others?
Do you have meaningful engagements with others?
Do your social interactions reflect peace, love and harmony?
Do you care about those around you?
Are you directly or indirectly making a difference in anyone's life?
Are you giving in any areas where you are not expecting anything in return?
If you said No to most of the above, you will need to revisit your Key Life Success Indicators. We are called for a bigger purpose, and we will talk more about this in Chapter 10.

> There is nothing more powerful than repurposing your life and leading it intentionally to create the life you love living.

If you have taken time to reflect on all the questions in the tests above, you are closer to your truth. If you feel your life is out of alignment, the next section will help you take steps towards redefining what success truly means to you.

Some of you already know the truth deep inside but deny the reality and choose not to get off the hamster wheel. I lived that way for a long time, hoping I would at some point, adapt to a misaligned life. But it does not work that way. You get sucked deeper into the pit of discontentment and defeat. There is nothing more powerful than repurposing your life and leading it intentionally to create the life you love living.

NOTES

My Success Metrics SECTION II

5

The Solution

In the last chapter, you assessed your life and have a fairly clear idea of where you stand in terms of your Key Life Success Indicators. The first step to getting from where you are to where you want to be is to know exactly where you are. This first step of awareness is a big stride in getting back in the right direction of creating and following your own best Success Path in alignment with your design.

If your assessment brought on the realization that you are in the right place, then you can start taking responsibility for your happiness and fulfillment right where you are. You can cultivate an attitude of gratitude for all that you have, choose to show up as your best self daily, without chasing, in vain, the life you think you are supposed to have. Even if you don't feel your life is out of alignment, this section can still take you through different stages of self-discovery.

> The first step to getting from where you are to where you want to be is to know exactly where you are.

If the assessment in the previous chapter revealed that your Key Life Success Indicators are misplaced and you need help breaking away from the conventional attitude towards success, then this section will help you unmask some hidden layers in your life and dig deep into your true self.

Regardless, Section III will help you create your unique personal roadmap to reach your Key Success Indicators.

The answer is within you
The good news is that you have the solution within yourself. Stop searching all over for answers. You don't need another guru, book, seminar or program to tell you who you really are and how your success path should look like. They may guide you, but you have everything you need, to be what you were created to be and to design a life you love living. Deep within, you already know the answers!

What this section will do

This section provides practical step-by-step guides that include powerful strategies and success principles to help you rewire your faulty patterns of thinking and cultivate an unstoppable mindset. It will take you on a journey of deeper awareness of who you are at your core, your true values, purpose and desires. These will become part of your Personal Manifesto. Embracing your whole true self will help you to take a step out of your space, if toxic, or to recreate your current space into a place of growth and inspiration.

That will help you to take a step out of your toxic space or recreate your current space into a place of growth and inspiration.

This process will take time and there are no quick fixes or hacks, but it will be a sweet journey where you will ultimately experience deep fulfillment, and passion in your daily life. I strongly recommend you

> MANIFESTO Take time to read through the different parts of your Personal Manifesto on Page 135. This is what you are going to build.

set aside at least thirty minutes for each chapter in this section.

There is no limit to the possibilities

You may be stuck in a mental space where you feel you have no way out, or you may have convinced yourself that you don't deserve any better or that it is too late. This section will open up your mind to the unlimited possibilities that are right in front of you. Just hang in there and be open to transformation at a deepest level as you go through each step to help you be who you were born to be.

"Your only limitation is the one you set up in your own mind!"

Napoleon Hill.

Whether your job, career, business, relationship, health, or your personal life, being authentic to who you are, your values and your purpose is the key to moving from a life of mediocrity to unleashing the incredible power within you. Redefining your Success Metrics is critical in moving from "settling" or "surviving" to "flourishing" and "thriving".

Living in such alignment will result in abundance and the resulting joy will overflow into other areas of your life. You will make a difference in the world around you and beyond.

6

Own Your Game

A critical step towards redefining your Key Life Success Indicators and creating your personal success path is to take full responsibility for your life. This chapter will give you practical steps on how to take back your power and rewrite your story.

"If you don't change what you are doing today, all of your tomorrows will look like yesterday" Jim Rohn

If you feel you have been climbing the wrong ladder, have lost what is most important to you in the process, and are seeking more fulfillment and meaning in your life, it's not too late to get down the ladder and get your life back in alignment with what truly matters to you. The worst thing you can do to yourself after realizing you are on the wrong ladder is to keep climbing higher, hoping things will get better. Such misplaced faith will lead you to irredeemable regrets.

If you want to optimize your strengths in your career, if you want to rebuild your relationship with your family, if you want to create wealth, if you want to give back to society or if you want to leave a legacy, it is up to you. The only thing stopping you from getting what you want is YOU. The only person limiting your growth, your dreams,

"If it's meant to be, it's up to me" Tom Dreeson

your productivity, and your impact is YOU! It's up to YOU!!!! Ask yourself, who is in charge of your life? Who is dictating your Success Metrics? Is your measurement of success based on expectations that others have from you? Do you feel you have no control over the direction your life is heading towards right now?

Blaming and complaining
I keep meeting people who blame their upbringing, past, parents, spouses, mothers-in-laws, or teachers for the life they are living. You position yourselves as a helpless victim as if you have no choice in what is happening in your life.

You always have a choice and it is yours to make.
Whether you have full support to follow your dreams or zero support, nobody can be blamed for where you are or where you end up in your journey. Nobody can make you do anything. You always have a choice.

Think about it. If somebody handed you a gun pointed at your child and threatened to kill you if you did not pull the trigger, what would you do? I know what I would do. If you are like most parents, you would choose to sacrifice your life before taking your child's life. And that proves the point. Even if you had a gun pointed at your head, the choice is yours. Nobody can make you do anything unless they actually manhandle you.

So, I decided to continue in the marriage while things continued deteriorating, affecting me physiologically, physically and mentally.

In my first marriage, I went through a lot of grief. I kept pretending all was well and hoped things would get better, but the pain just got worse. When the agony reached unbearable levels, I sought counsel from church leaders, much against the wishes of my ex-husband. Unfortunately, I got advice like, "Ignore for the sake of peace" and "Compromise". So, I decided to go on in the marriage though things continued deteriorating, affecting me physiologically and mentally. In hindsight, those are the worst pieces of advice to give anyone. A best friend of mine, who had a similar marital problem suffered a mental breakdown right in front of my eyes and eventually met an early demise after eight years of mental and physical anguish. That hit me hard. It was a wake-up call for me.

I realized I had to take responsibility for my life. I was at the point where I did not mind dying. If not for my faith and relationship with God, I probably would have taken my life. So, death did not bother me, but what scared me was going insane. I knew I could not blame it on the church leaders, religion or my ex-husband. Blaming would not change anything; it would not restore my sanity or give me back my life. My weight had gone down to 43 kgs (about 94 lbs.) and I would wail in my sleep. I realized that I had to take an action while I was still in a position to. Taking responsibility for my life helped me make decisions that changed my life.

People may oppose you and discourage you as you move towards your happiness. They may give you advice based on their limited experience and mindset. Before you take their advice to heart, ask yourself if they understood you and genuinely care for you.

I came to realize that the people who were advising me were not concerned about my well-being. My happiness and dreams meant nothing to them. One leader told me, "If you go for a divorce, others in the church will follow" and I had to carry the burden of others' marriages. I realized that even if I took their advice and stayed on in the marriage and ended up losing my sanity, they would not be there to support me. I had to face the consequences of my decisions.

If you have given over the responsibility of your life, your success and your happiness to somebody or something else, it's time to take it back.

If you have given over the responsibility of your life, your success, and your happiness to somebody or something else, it's time to take it back. If you have given control of your fate and future to somebody who has their own agenda and does not care for you, you may have to forcefully take back the controls of your life.

Once I did that, I was a brand-new person. The true me had been suppressed for so long in my marriage and I had been forced to be somebody who I wasn't. But when I took charge of my life, my health changed. People who had no idea about my personal life would ask me what made me look more alive. My true self finally found the freedom to emerge. Even people who were opposed to my divorce noticed that I had bloomed. I had successfully pretended to be happy for years, but the transformation they see in me now is not something I can pretend about.

"Destiny is not what is given to you but what you choose for yourself"

Megamind movie

Another thing to keep in mind is that no one owes you anything. If you do not create ways to reach your Success Metrics nobody else will do it for you. You cannot blame others for your failure to reach your dreams, for ending up sad and miserable, or for not achieving freedom in your life. It is up to you to take responsibility for yourself and the part you play in bringing the desired change in your life.

Stop saying, "My boss made me lie", "The company is killing my creativity", "My parents made me take engineering", "My job is causing me stress", "my wife made me late", "my children's college fees made me broke", "social media is robbing me of my peace", "the government makes me angry", etc. Nobody can have that control over you unless you allow it. Again, it is up to YOU!

I have to
You don't have to do anything that you don't want to do. It is a choice you make, based on what you believe is best for you and those who are important to you.

Once you understand that nobody can make you do anything and that you don't have to do anything you don't want to do, it is a shift from a victim mindset to a growth mindset.

You say I have to work. You don't have to. But being a wise person, you don't want to face the consequences of not having an income to support you and your family. Thus, you choose to go to work

You may say I have to pay the bills. The truth is, you don't have to pay the bills. But that choice will result in consequences of your services being disconnected, being fined, and other inconveniences. To avoid such, you 'choose' to pay your bills. Moreover, if you are paying bills, that means you are receiving services like water, electricity which is unavailable to a big part of the population in the world. So, in reality, you are privileged for the opportunity to be able to pay bills. You don't have to attend meetings, tolerate a cranky boss, pay taxes, keep the house clean or cook healthy meals. You choose to do it because you have a good enough reason to do it.

Once you understand that nobody can make you do anything and that you don't have to do anything you don't want to do, it is a shift from a victim mindset to a growth mindset. The victim mentality makes you believe that you have no control over what you do, and that life always just happens to you. It weakens your ability to make clear deliberate choices.

Think about the Key Life Success Indicators (KLSIs) you are following right now. Do you feel you have to be on the path you are on right now? Do you feel you have to quit and try a different path? You don't HAVE to do any of those! It is your choice! It is up to YOU!

QUICK TIP Rephrase your "I have to..." statements to "I choose to..." or "I get to..." statements.

The most important thing to remember is, whatever path you take, you are responsible for the consequences. Open your mind to this reality, as you create your Key Life Success Indicators. It is your choice to continue down the same path or to shift, pivot, or change the path. Take full responsibility for the consequences of your action or inaction.

It is your choice to continue down the same path or to shift, pivot, or change the path.

I Can't

"I can't "is another statement used by a lot by victim-minded people. The truth is, you can do whatever you have been saying you can't, but most often when you say, "I can't", you actually mean "I won't". If you say, "I can't ask for a promotion", you are saying you choose not to ask for a promotion, maybe to save yourself from an awkward conversation with your boss or from facing rejection.

You may be saying something like, "I can't swim". Well, you can learn to swim. It may take time, effort, investment in classes and will need you to get into the water. You can do whatever you want. It may be painful, uncomfortable, or even risky. And considering all those inconveniences, you have chosen not to swim. With the right tools, attitude, mindset, and motivation, the only thing holding you back is yourself. Besides, how can you know that you cannot swim unless you tried and failed. By saying, "I can't", you are submitting to defeat, sowing self-doubt, and putting a limit around your life. Thus, you are feeding negative signals to the brain that affects other areas of your life.

QUICK TIP Rephrase your "I can't.." statements to "I won't.." or "I choose not to.. " statements

Things you can control and things you cannot.
I came across this joke:

> **Tracy to her dietician:** What I am worried about is my height. I have no issues with my weight.
>
> **Dietician:** How come???
>
> **Tracy:** According to my weight, my height should be 7.8 feet.

I meet many people exactly like Tracy all the time. You may be saying "I have all it takes to succeed; I just wish I had a supportive and appreciative husband. "

"I have no problem with my skillset, my problem is the company's policies or the colleagues. That is why I am not performing well."

"I can build a business; my problem is I don't have the capital. I am just waiting to get that capital someday."

"My goals and priorities are in place, I just need five hours extra in a day, I just have so much to do. That is why I compromise on my health."

Like the height in the BMI formula, the equation of life has some constants and some variables. We have no control over the constants.

"There is no problem with me and my attitude, the problem is my boss/ mother-in-law/ husband/ children/ neighbor. That is the reason I am always unhappy, irritated or depressed."

Like the height in the BMI formula, the equation of life has some constants and some variables. We have no control over the constants. On the other hand, we can work on the variables - our responses, behavior, attitude, and personal development. Those are things we need to take responsibility for by taking action towards positive results. As with Tracy, blaming our bosses, spouse, the past, our family, our upbringing, the neighbors, the economy, lack of financial independence, technology or the government will not create the results you want. And some use such excuses to give up on themselves.

You may be deceived into thinking that you have no control over what is happening to you, or that you have no options. But, even in situations where you have zero control in being able to change the external environment, you do have maximum power in being able to shift your internal environment. You can reframe how you view

44

yourself, your roles and adjust your response to the situation and give it your best shot. And that can influence the outcomes, even when life throws you off balance.

When I worked as an HR consultant, I would have staff come to me complaining about how unhappy they were in their jobs. If you feel that your job does not bring you the satisfaction and growth that you are seeking, look for another job that will fit the bill. And if you are aware that finding another job is not easy, then be grateful for the one you have, shift your mindset, guard your peace, and put your best foot forward daily.

Don't let people, events, and circumstances around you dictate your state of mind, your peace, success or your future.

The worst thing you can do is to stay in a place that you detest and keep grumbling about it. Instead of complaining about things you cannot control, take steps towards things you can. Don't let people, events, and circumstances around you dictate your state of mind, your peace, success, or your future.

Conclusion
Once you understand that your life is your responsibility and you can create the results you want, you will be empowered to take your power back and recreate your story.

You can choose to stop blaming, complaining, justifying, defending, and excuse-making and own your game. You can get back in alignment with your Success Metrics, step into your purpose and live your life to the fullest potential. Stop waiting for somebody to come to rescue you, stop waiting for the right time to materialize, now is the time to get back into the driver's seat of your life and take your life in the direction you want it to go.

MANIFESTO

Craft bold statements of commitment in areas of your life that you want to take more responsibility for. Add how you want to improve your life for yourself, your family, and the world around you. Write them into your Personal Manifesto under "I declare/ commit to.." on Page 135.

45

Write down one of your life's 'WHAT IF's' or 'IF ONLY's?

What role did you play in creating or allowing that regret?

What would you do today differently to prevent future regrets?
I would:

Which area/ areas of your life do you want to take more responsibility for ?

What are some steps you can take to improve that area?

What can you do today?

DO IT NOW Take one step right now as an intentional move towards taking
responsibilty for one or more of the areas mentioned above.

7

Your True Beliefs

As explained in Chapter Three, we all have belief systems that are formed in our early childhood and teenage years influenced by our life experiences. Our belief systems, though subconscious, influence the way we see ourselves, the world around us, our behavior, and our motivation to create the life we desire.

Most people go through their lives never really feeling good about themselves and thinking that they are not enough. Your belief system makes you think you are broken, and you keep trying to fix yourself and, in the process, settle for a life way below your dreams.

This chapter will answer the question "Where am I?". It will help you to identify subconscious beliefs that are roadblocks to your future success and will give you steps to override them. It will also help you to embrace beliefs and life choices that genuinely resonate with who you are.

Locus of Control

There is a psychological concept worth mentioning, called the Locus of Control (LOC) which is an individual's belief system regarding the causes of his or her success or failure. The LOC refers to how strongly people believe they have control over the events and experiences that affect their lives. If you attribute your success to your hard work and choices, you have an internal locus of control and if you feel you have no control over what is happening or will happen, you have an external locus of control.

If you feel that regardless of what you do, your fate is decided by things not in your control, you will be less motivated to take action towards changing the situation.

There are several tests available online to identify your LOC. But the main takeaway is that if you feel that regardless of what you do, your fate is decided by things not in your control, you will be less motivated to take action towards changing the situation. This feeling of helplessness may lead to anxiety and stress. The LOC is not an inbuilt personality trait as it once was believed to be, but it is a conditioning "passed down" to us by the attitudes, beliefs, customs, traditions, and even religion of our caretakers. So, like any belief system, it can be rewired with time and practice.

Pain and pleasure

Human beings are hardwired to seek pleasure and avoid pain, but when faced with a choice between the two the brain will drive you to avoid pain, since survival is paramount.

For example, if you were offered a million dollars to spend a night in a hungry lion's den, you would most probably decline.

Human beings are hardwired to seek pleasure and avoid pain, but when faced with a choice between the two the brain will drive you to avoid pain, since survival is paramount.

So, if you have a limiting belief that an action may seemingly cause pain, your brain will keep you from taking steps in that direction, regardless of an end gain which could far outweigh the pain. So, if you experienced a negative outcome in the past from starting a business, your brain may prevent you from seeing opportunities that could lead you to be an entrepreneur, to protect you from pain. If you witnessed your parent always stressed and irritated because of their job, you may have an underlying distorted belief that work cannot bring joy.

Thus, your belief systems affect the way you perceive success and establish your Key Life Success Indicators for life. Even with the noblest of intentions, these subconscious inaccurate beliefs about self, success, reality, and life will cancel out what is truest to you.

Some common limiting beliefs

Below are some common sayings that we have heard growing up. We have accepted them as the gospel truth, and it affects the way we see and follow success. They are like mind viruses that spread into different areas of our life. They hold us back from being our best selves and creating the life we want.

- "You cannot teach old dogs new tricks" indicates your habits and negative thinking patterns cannot be changed.
- "Money is the root of all evil" - such beliefs can sabotage financial success.

- "Happiness is all about power, wealth, and fame" – can limit you from thinking outside the construct.
- "Everything will fall into place" may be interpreted as you don't need to take action to get the results you want.
- "You need a formal education to succeed" I am a huge proponent of education, but lack thereof should not stop you from reaching your dreams.
- "Quitting is losing" There is a difference between giving up and knowing when you have had enough or realizing that when something does not align with your true self.
- "I don't have time for …" Everybody has 24 hours. You can most certainly make time for what is most important to you.

I watched an animation recently where a young rabbit jumped off improperly from the second floor of a house and hit the ground.

"I cracked a rib!" he yelled, "How many ribs do we have?"

"13," was the reply.

"Sweet!!!!", he replied with a smile and climbed right back upstairs.

If you were the rabbit, what would your response be?

Response 1: I cracked a rib. Let me play safe. Let me avoid any more jumps. Let me not try anything new, I may hurt myself again.

Response 2: I have 12 ribs left. Let me try again, maybe I will get it right this time. There must be a better way to jump without getting hurt.

There is no right or wrong answer here. But the response will throw light on your belief system. It may reveal how your parents or guardians viewed failure and how you may respond to it.

Other beliefs that hinder us from thinking out of the box and defining our own Success Metrics:

"It is not possible to do what I love and become wealthy."

"Wealthy people are greedy, corrupt, self-centred and boastful."

"There's only ONE 'true' path to success."

"Life is hard, and it takes a lifetime to achieve success."

"The world is evil."

"Success will attract many false friends and true enemies."

"You have to change everything about yourself to reach your goals."

Some common limiting self-beliefs

There are some things you believe about yourself that may be detrimental to your growth and happiness. Most of these beliefs did not originate as your idea. It may have been planted in your subconscious by your parents, teachers, bosses, even spouses.

When you do not value yourself, you cannot expect others to value you.

- I'm not good enough/ I am not _____enough.
- Bad luck always follows me.
- I don't deserve happiness.
- If I follow my dreams, I am selfish.
- I'm too young/old/uneducated to do what I love.
- I am so ordinary.
- I am not able.
- Everybody should approve of me.

When you do not value yourself, you cannot expect others to value you. You live your life trying to please others and make others happy believing your passion, fulfillment, and dreams do not matter. For a long time in my first marriage, through repeated feedback from my ex-husband, I was convinced that I was not worthy. That nagging self-belief that I was not good enough made me give up on my dreams and my life for a long time. I convinced myself that I did not matter and what was important to me did not count. I meet women who believe that once they are married or have children their dreams become invalid. Sometimes, it may be necessary to sacrifice your passions for the sake of family, but continually giving without receiving back can drain your wellness reservoir.

Four Steps to Eliminate Limiting Beliefs
STEP 1- Identify the limiting beliefs:

The first step to overriding the disempowering beliefs is to be aware of them. Simply being aware of the limiting belief can minimize its effect on your life. You may have heard them for so long that you feel they are normal or that they are the absolute truth. In fact, some of them may sound well-meaning, but they hold you back in your work, business, home, and different areas of your life. Once you are aware of them, you can choose to change them!

Identify one or more limiting beliefs from the ones above, that you were conditioned to believe. Think of any self-defeating beliefs that have held you back in your life. Write them down below:

My Limiting Beliefs

We will address one belief at a time during this process of eliminating limiting beliefs. Turn to the My Beliefs Worksheet on Page 54 and write one of the above limiting beliefs in Section 1 of the worksheet.

STEP 2- Dismantle the old belief:
The next step is to dismantle the old belief by finding evidence that contradicts it. These beliefs have been ingrained within you and it is hard to just dismiss them. Actively seeking evidence that invalidates the belief, will make the subconscious mind question the belief thereby helping in undoing the belief. Any belief can be changed if you question it enough. Once you find that you can't prove these limiting beliefs to be true, beyond a shadow of doubt, you can decide to discard them. Answer 2-5 in the Worksheet.

STEP 3- Replace the old belief with empowering beliefs:

Beliefs are like the legs of a table. When you discard one, replacing it with another belief will help you to gain stability and not revert to the old belief. So, the next step is to build up a new counter-belief. With the old belief in mind, answer 6 & 7 in the worksheet

STEP 4- Create an empowering affirmation:

Some examples of affirming statements:
I am more than enough.
I can do anything I set my mind to.
I am destined for succuss.
The world is a beautiful place and I am playing my part in making it beautiful.
I am changing my thoughts, words and action to create.

Affirmations are positive declarations that assert who you are, your beliefs, and how you experience life. These affirmations, when repeated over and over again, affect your emotions and penetrates to the depths of your subconscious minds to replace past beliefs. It helps in rewiring the neural pathways in your brain in such a way that your response to the same situation eventually changes to a constructive one. Take the new belief that you wrote in Setion 6 and craft it into a strong affirmative statement and write it in Section 8.

The examples of empowering affirmations in the box on the left will give you ideas to create your own.

QUICK TIP Check out a live example of the 'Four Steps to Eliminate Eliminating Limiting Beliefs' on Page 53, to help you through your steps

Repeat STEPS 1-4 for each limited belief that you wrote in STEP 1. You can group similar beliefs together if you like. You will end up with affirmations of new beliefs.

MANIFESTO When you are satisfied with the phrasing of the affirmations of your new beliefs, enter the top two into "I believe.." of the Manifesto on Page 135.

Conclusion

Overriding your self-defeating beliefs will help open your mind to unlimited possibilities of success, joy, and fulfillment, without confining yourself to the cultural constructs of success. Awareness of such beliefs, replacing them with empowering ones, and combining them with the subtle force of repeated suggestions, will help you develop an unstoppable mindset that will transform your life.

Four Steps to Eliminate Limiting Beliefs
Step 1 - Identity your self-limiting belief:
"I am too old to change my career field or start a new business"

EXAMPLE

Step 2 - Dismantle the old belief:
Where did the idea come from? Is it true?

That idea comes from my culture. I don't see women in their forties try out new ventures. Their life mostly revolves around their children and family and their dreams are not given importance.

What fears did you develop because of it? In what way did it limit you?

I thought it was too late to pursue my dreams and utilize my gifts and ideas. I feared thinking out of the box and exploring new ventures. The feeling of inadequacy limited me from supporting people in need.

Are you absolutely sure about this phrase? No

Write down 3 examples in your life (or others) that disprove the belief.

There are many women who have established empires, starting in their forties. I have done many things in my forties that are not common for ladies this age. My strength and determination have been demonstrated through my life experiences.

Step 3 - Replace the old belief with empowering beliefs
New Empowering Belief: It is not too late to start something new.
Evidence of new belief:

Martha Steward did not start writing books until she was already in her 40s, Colonel Sander started KFC at 65, JK Rowling kickstarted her career as a writer at 32, Reid Hoffman founded LinkedIn at 35, Morgan Freeman was 50 when he landed his first big break.

Step 4 - Create an empowering affirmation
I am more than capable of pursuing any new venture I want to at any age. I am not too old to accomplish what I want to.

My Beliefs Worksheet

Fill this out for each limiting belief you have.

STEP 1

1. WRITE DOWN ONE LIMITING BELIEF.

STEP 2

2. WHERE DID THIS IDEA COME FROM? IS IT TRUE?

3. WHAT FEARS DID YOU DEVELOP BECAUSE OF THEM? HOW DID IT LIMIT YOU

4. ARE YOU SURE ABOUT THE BELIEF?

5. CAN YOU FIND EVIDENCE IN YOUR LIFE THAT DISPROVES THIS BELIEF. WRITE DOWN 3 EXAMPLES.

STEP 3

6. WRITE DOWN A COUNTER-BELIEF THAT YOU WOULD LIKE TO HOLD INSTEAD.

7. WRITE DOWN EVIDENCE THAT THAT SUPPORTS THE NEW EMPOWERING BELIEF YOU WANT TO HAVE?

STEP 4

8. WRITE AN EMPOWERING AFFIRMATION FOR THIS NEW BELIEF.

8

Your True Identity

"Who are you?"

If Iasked you that question, what would your answer be? Please pause for a moment and answer that question.

Most often, the response to such a question would be related to a predominant function or focus of awareness. So, you would probably say, I am a (profession), I am a wife/husband, I am a man/woman, I am single/divorced, I am a Republican/Democrat and the like.

But I want you to do this. Look at yourself closely in the mirror (or on the selfie mode of your camera). Take a good look at each part of your face, the cheeks, the eyes, and the iris, and ask yourself, looking at the mirror as an observer, "Who are you?" This is a deeper question between you and yourself. Are you just the body that you are looking at? Is the real you somewhere within the body? These questions are not meant to extract a fixed black-and-white answer, rather it is intended to provoke your curiosity of self.

"Who am I?", is a life-defining question that reveals your identity. Your sense of identity affects the way you experience life, from the choices you make to the way you respond to situations.

You may have achieved everything you dreamed of but are still unhappy. You may have everything you need and want, but still feel a lack. One reason for this is that you are not living in integrity with your true self. It is possible that you do not know who you are and have applied inaccurate labels to yourself. This leads to unhappiness, unfulfillment and emptiness.

> Your sense of identity affects the way you experience life, from the choices you make to the way you respond to situations.

This chapter is intended to increase your self-awareness and bring you closer to knowing your true identity. That way, you can align your success markers in a way that is authentic to you.

The discovery of the 'I' is the fundamental experience of awareness of oneself and that is what distinguishes us from animals. Experiments have shown how questions related to your identity and values, activate a part of your brain called the ventromedial prefrontal cortex, which helps us make better decisions. So, to set authentic Key Life Success Indicators for your life, understanding yourself is a good starting point.

The influence

Through our childhood and life experiences, we have a constant input of influence on our identity from our environment. The beliefs and values of our parents, caretakers, and dominant cultures veil the clarity of consciousness and can produce false identifications of the self. So, you don't choose your identity; it is imposed on you or demanded from you and you associate yourself with an identity that is not aligned with your true self and that can cause a lot of unfulfillment and stress.

Identifying solely with your role can get you trapped into settling for a life that is not in line with what you were placed on Earth for.

That question of who you are may pop up sometimes, but you generally identify yourself with that which seems to you to be most real, or most intense at that time. Most often, it is the predominant role you play - at work, business, or home. Maybe husband/wife, mother/father, a manager, boss, housewife or student. You identify yourself with that role, and you live, function, and experience yourself in terms of that role. The reality is that you are more than the role you play. Identifying solely with your role can get you trapped into settling for a life that is not in line with what you were placed on Earth for. Others identify themselves with their bodies, minds, beliefs, gender, nationality, religion, political affiliations, sexual orientations marital status, and such.

You play multiple roles

Further, we play multiple roles, so a continuing identification with a predominant role can result in an identity crisis, where a person does not recognize themselves anymore when there is a shift in that role or function. Such identity crises take place when a woman who has been married most of her life suddenly finds herself divorced or widowed; or a man who has identified himself as a professional all his life loses his job; an actress whose physical beauty fades; a wealthy person who loses all his possessions. Such entrapment in single identities gives people a false sense of security and you cease to see any value in yourself without your job, job title, marriage, office, children, etc. Setting your Key Life Success Indicators conforming to such identities leads to unhappiness, depression, grief, and meaninglessness. A friend of mine, who was a full-time home-maker and mother, shared with me how she recently found herself lost after her son left for college. She has to recraft her identity and repurpose her life to adjust to the shift in role. This is an example where clinging on to 'expired' identities can be futile.

Your interpretation of a role

Another thing to note is that your interpretation of the role you play is based on your exposure to that role, and you form an identity for yourself based on what you believe is the right way to execute that role. A neural association is created in your brain, regarding what a mother, father, boss, wife, husband, a divorcee should be like.

On a subconscious level, you do not want to fall out of the mainstream thinking regarding the role, even if that thinking may not align with who you really are

If your mother sacrificed her career to raise and nurture her children, you may blame yourself for pursuing your career and leaving your kids with the nanny, if something went wrong. On the other hand, if you had a working mother who successfully balanced work and family, you may associate that as normal and may feel inadequate if you gave up your career for the children. On a subconscious level, you do not want to fall out of the mainstream thinking regarding the role, even if that thinking may not align with who you really are

So, your subconscious understanding of these identities is based on the feedback from your environment and it could be flawed, thus leading to discontent. If you have been exposed to the role of a boss as someone mean and arrogant, then you may subconsciously avoid opportunities that can land you a promotion to become a boss. Alternatively, you may end up being a boss, but never really enjoy that position. You will need to break that negative association with the idea of bosses to foster satisfaction at work.

You may have seen your father as an emotionless disciplinarian and believe that that is how a father should be, even though you are not like that at the core. You may have seen your mother give up her dreams even when she had a chance to pursue them and you subconsciously exclude your personal passions in your Success Metrics. While some of these identities help you in your journey, you need to learn to glean the good. Many of the identities that you hold on to can limit you from connecting with your true self and living your best life. Also, remember that each person is wired uniquely, and it is essential to embrace your true self unapologetically.

You have multiple identities
You also need to remember that not only do you play multiple roles, you are multi-dimensional human being with multiple identities. Holding on to just one identity, excludes or greatly decreases your experience in other aspects of your being and will prevent you from living life to its full extent. The label you give yourself is tragically limited and can act as a boundary that you set up for yourself.

What you identify with most intensely and intentionally controls you.

Your identity controls you
What you identify with most intensely and intentionally controls you. If you identify more strongly as a woman than a human being, you will find yourself taking any negative women-related comment personally. You may strongly identify with your possession, job, hobby, or a cause you are following. It gets you attention, makes you feel important and gives you a feeling of self-worth and security. In such cases, you may resist or avoid change, even if the change will improve your life, because the issue you are trying to address has become interwoven with your self-identity.

When I was married, I was working as an engineer. My identity was wife and engineer. I had some inclination to the arts, but my ex-husband was against me doing anything unrelated to engineering. And I accepted the primary identity of an engineer. Then when I became a mother, that was another role I added to my identity. As a side note, in Uganda, when you give birth, you are no longer called by your name, but by the name of your first child. So, I was Mama Evangeline. The marriage was dysfunctional and when I felt like a failure in my identity as a wife, I devoted myself to being the best mother. Even when the marriage was degenerating, I fought on. And I had held on to another strong identity through my religion. Being a Christian, divorce is shunned upon and the religious leaders made it clear that living in an unhappy, painful marriage was more important than living happily out of it. I was ready to sacrifice the true Edlyn for my marriage, for the sake of my kids and religion. I did not care about who I really was, beyond a wife, mother, an engineer, and a Christian.

At my lowest point, when I was seeking answers, I got a divine revelation where I felt God telling me that I was more than all the identities I had limited myself to. I was His child, His creation and my life was very precious to Him. The restoration of my self-worth helped me to break the identity limits I had set. Leaving my engineering career, and starting a freelance business was another shift in identity. I chose to follow that path because as much as an engineering career gave me a sense of status, it did not align with my true self.

By discovering your true self, underneath the hidden layers and living a life authentic to you, you will be able to align your outer realities with your inner needs

This chapter will help you uncover your identity and question the identity labels that do not serve you in achieving your true Success Metrics. By discovering your true self, underneath the hidden layers and living a life authentic to you, you will be able to align your outer realities with your inner needs. It will also help you derive meaning in the depth of interconnectedness that unites us as humans.

The good news is that since most elements of your identity were created or applied and are not part of your genetic makeup, your identity can be recreated to serve you better. You have the power to choose which aspects of your identity you want to keep and those you want to discard. Once you have accepted your true identity, you have the freedom to disidentify from any aspect of your being that limits you and negatively controls you while uncovering and creating a new identity that will facilitate and foster growth and help you live your best self.

The great Italian sculptor and painter Michelangelo, once said, "In every block of marble I see a statue as plain as though it stood before me, shaped and perfect in attitude and action. I have only to hew away the rough walls that imprison the lovely apparition to reveal it to the other eyes as mine see it."

When you look at your life, from the vantage point of a detached observer, you can gain a clearer understanding of what is hidden underneath.

Michelangelo saw the treasure within each unshaped, ragged block of marble he worked on. He once described the process this way, "I saw the angel in the marble and carved until I set him free." He could do this because he didn't see what the marble was, he saw what the marble would be. When you look at your life, from the vantage point of a detached observer, you can gain a clearer understanding of what is hidden underneath.

The steps below will help you peel off the layers and dig deep into your self-consciousness to uncover your true self. Set aside time and space without any distraction so you can dig deep.

STEP 1- Awareness:

At the start of this chapter, I posed the question, "Who are you?" Whatever your answer may have been, take some time to reflect on it before we proceed. When you start asking the questions below, you will start seeing patterns that will help you become intimately aware of your identity, and unveil who you are at your core. Turn to the My Identity Worksheet on Page 65 and ask yourself the following questions:

What do you spend most of your time on?

What do you talk about most?

Where do you spend most of your resources? On whom?

What does your friend-circle/environment look like?

Do you see a healthy balance in your life with the identities you hold?

Do you have to be pretentious most times or are you free to be your true self wherever you are?

Are you accepting of different opinions and views?

Are you leaving room for new ideas, experiences?

What causes are you most passionate about?

These questions will help you understand what you identify as most.

Based on your answers, write down who you think you are in Section 1 of the worksheet. E.g., wife, father, businessman, beautiful, strong, rich, professional, single, divorced, woman, creative, boring, gay, Christian, generous, lazy, worthless, feminist, etc.

Of these, circle the ones that were obtained from or influenced by your parents, caretakers, family, or other social influences.

Our identity influences the people we relate to and where we spend our time, energy and focus. If your identity is based solely on your education or job, you may only have friends who are working and educated and find it hard to relate to uneducated or people from the lower strata. If you mostly identify with your political affiliation or religion, you may knowingly or unknowingly develop a dislike towards people of other views or beliefs.

Our identity influences the people we relate to and where we spend our time, energy and focus.

In Section 2 of the worksheet, write down identities from Section 1 that inspire you. These are identities you would want to maintain.

"You must first be who you really are, then do what you need to do, in order to have what you want." —Margaret Young

STEP 2- What you are not:

The first part of the disidentification process is to be aware of the identities you want to discard. This section includes a self-reflective exercise that will help you get a deeper sense of self by verifying what you are not. This is especially helpful if you feel that a particular identity is controlling you and limiting your progress.

You are not what you do- That is your occupation/profession. It pays your bills and you do it to support yourself and your family. So, you may work as a teacher or a therapist, or run a business or manage the home, but that is not who you are.

You are not your role- You may be a mother, father, brother, daughter, or husband, but that is not the entirety of who you are.

You are not what you have- When you let your possessions and accomplishments define who you are, you may lack contentment within. That is because even if you achieve everything you set out to, there is more to chase. What you have is not who you are.

61

You are not your problems- You may have gone through adversities, you may be a survivor of sickness, or maybe challenged physically or mentally. That is not who you are. If you are clinging on to that identity, you may have a Victim Identity (more about the Victim Identity on Page 64)

You are not your past- Your past has a great influence on your being, but if any identity related to your past holds you back, you can choose to discard that identity.

Additionally, you are not your race, tribe, sexual orientation, political affiliations, nationality, religion, gender or emotional state.

As you identify identities that are misaligned with your true self that need to be shed, enter them into Section 3 of the Worksheet.

Now that you are starting to identify what you are not, let us dig further into your self-consciousness and become clearly aware of the thoughts, feelings, hopes, and fears that have been linked to any other identities with the following questions:

Is there a label you hold on to that is not true to who you really are?

Are there any identities that do not add meaning and fulfillment to your life?

Is any identity holding you back from being all that you are capable of being?

Do you have identities that are potential roadblocks to your growth and progress?

Do you have identities that oppose inclusivity and harmony?

If yes, add those identities to Section 3 of the Worksheet.

STEP 3- Disidentification:

Once you are aware of the identities that you want to shed, you can begin with the disidentification process.

Read the following:

Step outside of yourself and look at yourself as an observer. Remember Michelangelo with this block of marble. Envision your true self, your "I" as your center of consciousness inside the block, and the identities you want to shed as part of the outer marble block. Envision yourself chipping away at them, one by one as you see the beautiful YOU emerge. As a detached observer, try to recognize identities that do not serve you and how they are attached to you. Note that some identities may be easier to chip away than others.

Now, close your eyes, take a few breaths, and visualize what you read above. Take your time. This is a deep transformational process. Now open your eyes. Read the statements below and write your own statements in accordance with the identities you want to discard (from Section 3) into Section 4 of the My Identity Worksheet.

Being a _____ is a role I play. That is not who I am

_____ is my profession. That is not who I am.

_____ is my marital status. That is not who I am.

_____ is my gender. That is not who I am.

_____ is my nationality/ religion. That is not who I am.

I possess a _____ That is not what defines me.

In the same way, disidentify from any other function, roles, affiliations, marital status, experiences, pains, disability, overpowering emotions, material possessions, accomplishments, fame, and any other identities that hold you back from living your fullest life. Declare them as you write them down.

When you discard all the misaligned identities, what remains is your essence, a center of pure self-awareness which takes you closer to your true 'I', the center of true identity. Repeat this process if needed.

STEP 4- New identity:

Once you have completed the disidentification process, it's time to create a new strong identity for yourself. You can now see yourself beyond who you had limited yourself to be. Building on who you are, there is no limit on who you can become. You can add success qualities that resonate with you to your identity to make your life more purposeful and impactful.

The starting point is the identities you mentioned in Section 2 that you want to maintain and develop. These identities bring meaning and joy to your life.

The questions in Phase II of the Identity Worksheet will help you identify any other powerful success identities that you would like to embody.

Write down names of people you admire and would want to be like in Section 5 of the worksheet. In Section 6, write down their personal

> When you discard all the misaligned identities, what remains is your essence, a center of pure self-awareness which takes you closer to your true 'I', the center of true identity.

qualities that drew you to them, e.g., brave, authentic, wise, humble, inspiring, grateful, purposeful, strong, etc.

Now craft a statement of your new identity using answers from Sections 2 and 6 and write it down with conviction in Section 7. E.g. I am a strong and compassionate woman and a kind human being.

MANIFESTO Enter your Identity Statement into your Personal Manifesto on Page 135 under "I am ..".

Once you have created a new empowering identity, release it and allow a new sense of self to flow. Test this new identity with the new experiences that you have.

Revisit this chapter as you navigate through life and repeat the exercise as needed to remind you of your true identity. Letting go of who you think you are and embracing who you really are will result in a state of flow and a great sense of aliveness.

Conclusion

Discovering who you are is the gateway to understanding what matters most to you. That will enable you to set your Key Life Success Indicators in a way that is authentic to you. Understanding that there are no limits to becoming who you want to be will open you up to experiences that expand who you are, and to embrace life with all the beauty it presents in a whole new light.

Victim Identity

There is another identity that many people unknowingly hang on to that is worth mentioning. That is the Identity of Victim/Lack. You may have gone through some painful experiences. It is part of your story and it hurt so much that you start believing that is part of who you are. You become so attached to your pain/lack that part of you resists letting go of those things that make you unhappy. If you are always talking about how bad your job is or how abusive your partner is, how being single is lonely, it maybe be because you believe you are someone who is always a victim - helpless and at the mercy of others. Such a mindset will make it difficult for you to remove yourself from a toxic or painful space and take action towards leading a life that truly matters to you.

A quick test to see if you have a victim identity:

· Do you feel you are never in control of what is happening to you?
· Do you feel you always are at the mercy of others to live the life you want?
· Do you feel others (partner, children, boss) are responsible for your happiness?
· Do you talk a lot about a particularly traumatic or painful identity- Job/marriage/ disability/ problem/
· Do you get attention because of it?
· Do you feel attached to it and cannot let it go?

If most of your answers are yes, you may have a Victim Mindset. Go back to Chapter 6, which will inspire and empower you to take more responsibility for your life and create a growth mindset.

My Success Metrics · My Identity Worksheet

Phase I : AWARENESS

1. WHO AM I?

CIRCLE THE ONES THAT WERE OBTAINED FROM OR INFLUENCED BY YOUR PARENTS, FAMILY OR SOCIAL INFLUENCES.

2. IDENTITIES YOU WANT TO MAINTAIN:

Phase I : DISIDENTIFICATION

3. IDENTITIES YOU WANT TO DISCARD - WHAT I AM NOT, LIMITING IDENTITIES

4. WRITE YOUR PERSONAL DISIDENTIFICATION STATEMENTS

Phase II: NEW IDENTITY

5. WHO ARE THE PEOPLE YOU WANT TO EMULATE ?

6. WHAT ARE SOME OF THEIR PERSONAL QUALITIES THAT YOU LIKE MOST?

7. NEW IDENTITY STATEMENT

I am a

NOTES

9

Your True Values

On your journey of self-discovery and defining your Key Life Success Indicators, another vital guiding factor is your value system.

Your value system is the set of fundamental beliefs that influence how you live your life. It says a lot about the kind of person you are and what is important to you. It plays a critical role in your day-to-day decisions and when you are required to make difficult choices.

If your Success Metrics are not aligned with your values, you will feel guilt, restlessness, emptiness, and dissatisfaction even if you seemingly have it all. When you don't honor your values, knowingly or unknowingly, your physical state suffers too, in addition to your mental and emotional state.

For example, if you value integrity and end up as the Chief Finance Officer of a company that expects you to misappropriate funds, your conscience may torment you. If you value creativity and learning, then working in an environment with rigid systems may cause you to feel stifled, even if you had an envious job title and salary scale. No achievement or accomplishment is worth sacrificing your values.

> If your Success Metrics are not aligned with your values, you will feel guilt, restlessness, emptiness, and dissatisfaction even if you seemingly have it all.

You will experience greater meaning and fulfillment when you live by your values. If you constantly experience a lot of discontent and inner conflict, you may need to re-evaluate your Key Life Success Indicators and align them with your set of core values.

How do I know my true values?
We acquire many of our values from our parents, caregivers, culture, or religious leaders. You may still be living by some of them, but your set of core values will have changed as you matured, based on how you experienced life and the personal lessons you learned from the world around you.

67

Values cannot be chosen, they are integral to who you are and need to be discovered.

This section will provide step-by-step instructions to discover your core values and get more clarity around them. Remember, this is another soul-searching exercise. Values cannot be chosen; they are integral to who you are and need to be discovered. Again, there is no get-your-value-quick formula. So be patient and take your time to do this exercise. Most of all, be honest with yourself. Turn to the My Values Worksheet on Page 71 for this exercise.

STEP 1- Brainstorming:
Read the following questions and write down your thoughts as they flow in Section 1 of the worksheet. There is no right or wrong answer.
- What matters most to you?
- What qualities do my colleagues/bosses/family members appreciate you for? What is different about you?
- What do you not tolerate at work or home?
- Think about the bigger world news, social media, world events. What bothers you, what inspires you, what makes your heart smile?
- What makes you feel accomplished?
- What words do you want to live your life by?
- What makes you feel conflicted?

STEP 2- Values you admire in others:
a. Who are the people you admire or love, maybe people you know or some famous historical figure? Write down their names in Section 2 of the worksheet. E.g. your teacher, grandparent, a politician, a famous scientist, businessman, etc.
b. Write down the principles that drove them or what was most important to them in Section 3 of the worksheet. E.g., honesty, family, health, education, discipline, integrity, excellence, etc.

STEP 3- List of values
Check the list of values on Page 70 and see if any echo with what you have listed in Sections 1 and 3 in the worksheet. Write down any other values that are revealing themselves? This list is a guideline and just a starting point. Don't let it limit you. You can add other values that are not on the list.

Note: Do not select values that sound good or are seemingly more honorable. You are not trying to impress or please anybody.

STEP 4- Identify a theme:
Look through all the values listed in Section 4 and see if you can identify any pattern emerging. Group together related ones into one and write the grouping in Section 5 of the Worksheet.

STEP 5- Life choices:
Think back upon your past experiences and pick 3-4 top value groups from Section 5 that seem to resonate with them and enter them in Section 6. If you have ever experienced an unexplainable inner conflict in the past when making choices that compromised certain values, that value group should be on top of your list.

STEP 6- Revise after observation
Now that you have a draft list of your core value groups, observe your life for a week and see if there are values to add or remove from the list. Be mindful of the daily choices you make at home, work, running errands, etc., and note the value groups that are consistent with your lifestyle. If you feel conflicted and dissatisfied, not living by certain values, note that too.

At the end of the week, write down your final list of 4-5 value groups in Section 7 of the worksheet. Keep revisiting your values and go through these steps again regularly to redefine and refine your values in line with your true self, as needed.

MANIFESTO Enter your top 4-5 values into your Personal Manifesto under "My Core Values are .." or Page 135.

Conclusion
Knowing your values is a gateway to self-knowledge. Once you have clear core values defined, you can assess whether your present Key Life Success Indicators are in alignment with them or if your KLSIs belong to somebody else. Setting goals and actions consistent with your values will prevent you from getting in your own way.

List of Values**

Acceptance	Cooperation	Fun	Moderation	Simplicity
Accomplishment	Courage	Generosity	Motivation	Sincerity
Accountability	Courtesy	Genius	Openness	Skill
Accuracy	Creation	Giving	Optimism	Skillfulness
Achievement	Creativity	Goodness	Order	Smart
Adaptability	Credibility	Grace	Organization	Solitude
Alertness	Curiosity	Gratitude	Originality	Spirit
Altruism	Decisive	Greatness	Passion	Spirituality
Ambition	Decisiveness	Growth	Patience	Spontaneous
Amusement	Dedication	Happiness	Peace	Stability
Assertiveness	Dependability	Hard work	Performance	Status
Attentive	Determination	Harmony	Persistence	Stewardship
Awareness	Development	Health	Playfulness	Strength
Balance	Devotion	Honesty	Poise	Structure
Beauty	Dignity	Honor	Potential	Success
Boldness	Discipline	Hope	Power	Support
Bravery	Discovery	Humility	Present	Sustainability
Brilliance	Drive	Imagination	Productivity	Talent
Calm	Effectiveness	Improvement	Professionalism	Teamwork
Candor	Efficiency	Independence	Prosperity	Temperance
Capable	Empathy	Individuality	Purpose	Thankful
Careful	Empower	Innovation	Quality	Thorough
Certainty	Endurance	Inquisitive	Realistic	Thoughtful
Challenge	Energy	Insightful	Reason	Timeliness
Charity	Enjoyment	Inspiring	Recognition	Tolerance
Cleanliness	Enthusiasm	Integrity	Recreation	Toughness
Clear	Equality	Intelligence	Reflective	Traditional
Clever	Ethical	Intensity	Respect	Tranquility
Comfort	Excellence	Intuitive	Responsibility	Transparency
Commitment	Experience	Irreverent	Restraint	Trust
Common sense	Exploration	Joy	Results-oriented	Trustworthy
Communication	Expressive	Justice	Reverence	Truth
Community	Fairness	Kindness	Rigor	Understanding
Compassion	Family	Knowledge	Risk	Uniqueness
Competence	Famous	Lawful	Satisfaction	Unity
Concentration	Fearless	Leadership	Security	Valor
Confidence	Feelings	Learning	Self-reliance	Victory
Connection	Ferocious	Liberty	Selfless	Vigor
Consciousness	Fidelity	Logic	Sensitivity	Vision
Consistency	Focus	Love	Serenity	Vitality
Contentment	Foresight	Loyalty	Service	Wealth
Contribution	Fortitude	Mastery	Sharing	Winning
Control	Freedom	Maturity	Significance	Wisdom
Conviction	Friendship	Meaning	Silence	Wonder

**This list is from https://scottjeffrey.com/core-values-list/ compiled by Scott Jeffrey. To go deeper into discovering your values, I would recommend the resources available on his site especially the Core Values Workshop Course - https://scottjeffrey.com/values-workshop/

My Values Worksheet

1. BRAINSTORMING

2. WRITE DOWN THE NAMES OF PEOPLE YOU ADMIRE?

3. WHAT MAIN PRINCIPLES GUIDE/GUIDED THEIR LIVES?

4. CHECK THE VALUE LIST AND WRITE DOWN ANY THAT ARE IN LINE WITH THOSE IN 1 & 3

5. IDENTIFY A THEME IF ANY AMONG THE VALUES LISTED IN 4 AND GROUP THEM.

6. IF YOU HAVE MORE THAN 4 LISTED ABOVE, SELECT 3-4 BASED ON ANY CONNECTION WITH LIFE CHOICE IN THE PAST?

7. REVISE AFTER A WEEK OF OBSERVATION AND WRITE DOWN FINAL LIST

NOTES

10

Your True Purpose

"Definiteness of purpose is the starting point of all achievement."
W. Clement Stone

Another key to defining your Key Life Success Indicators and mapping out your personal Success Path is knowing your purpose. This chapter will build on your beliefs, identity and values you uncovered in the past chapters and take you through different steps to help you discover the unique purpose of your life.

"Why am I here?"
This is a question that has been asked for generations, by people at different stages of life. You seek answers in your jobs, communities, relationships, causes, and cultures. You may live life on default mode, but deep inside you know you were made for something significant. You have been put on earth for a specific purpose that is part of something bigger than yourself and you innately are seeking that throughout your life

"The mystery of human existence lies not in just staying alive, but in finding something to live for." Fyodor Dostoyevsky

Live life by your design
Consider for a moment, an advanced model of a scientific calculator. Its purpose is to accomplish complicated mathematical computations. However, if it is given to a fourth-grader, he would probably use it for simple additions and subtractions.

If you were part of the designing and manufacturing of that calculator and had spent endless hours developing its complex functions, I am sure you would be disappointed to see your precious creation used as a toy. In the same way, our Maker feels the same disappointment when you play small with your potential.

It is tragic for a sophisticated tool to be used for a way lower function than what it was designed for. But the biggest tragedy is that majority of the people around the world are living that way. And you may be one of them. Instead of thinking out of the box and setting extraordinary Key Life Success Indicators (KLSIs) in line with your purpose, you have succumbed to the general success standards of the world.

> Our Creator has a unique design for you, and you owe it to Him to be a good steward of the gifts that been given to you

Our Creator has a unique design for you, and you owe it to Him to be a good steward of the gifts that been given to you. But instead of living your purpose, you are stuck in your comfort zone, settling for an average career, average happiness, average relationships, average productivity, average performance and average quality of life. That is indeed very tragic.

The problem is not that the scientific calculator cannot compute 5+ 5. It absolutely can. But it was not designed for that and when you live lower than your design, you are wasting your potential. Our Creator may be looking at some of us and pitying our lack of capacity utilization. You are not designed for the ordinary. It may look different for different people, but you are designed for extraordinary. Each one of you has a superhero, a warrior, a high performer, a game-changer inside you. But if you want to live an overall meaningful life without regrets, it is up to YOU. You need to take a step into your true greatness, it is your responsibility. You need to own your purpose and redefine your personal Success Metrics in line with it.

"The graveyard is the richest place on earth because it is here that you will find all the hopes and dreams that were never fulfilled, the books that were never written, the songs that were never sung, the inventions that were never shared, the cures that were never discovered, all because someone was too afraid to take that first step, keep with the problem, or determined to carry out their dream." Les Brown

You dim your light

By living lower than your design, you dim your light and deprive others of benefiting from what you have to offer. Each one of you has a host of talents and gifts within you, but you don't utilize them. Instead, you spend your lifetime fixing your weakness or developing what you don't have. When you do not serve your purpose or misuse your gifts, they lose their sharpness. That is sad.

> By living lower than your design, you dim your light and deprive others of benefiting from what you have to offer.

Everyone has a role to play in the world

In an orchestra, different musicians play different instruments, each person playing a unique part. The individual music may not sound extraordinary, but when each one of them come together, the result is magical.

There is a master plan that includes the seating and positioning. Some of the performers are more visible roles than others, some sounds you hear are louder while others are softer. The smaller and softer instruments may seem unimportant, but each instrument and musician, has significance in the master plan. Without each person playing his part, at the right place at the right time, the orchestra cannot be a success. In the same way, when each person brings their unique skills, talents, and passions to the table, great things happen, and they create a life of abundance and meaning.

For some, their purpose and impact may be visibly spectacular but for others, it may not look like much. Some were created for talking, coaching, managing, or teaching; others creating, nurturing, or supporting. Whatever it may be, when you do what you were created to do, when you align your activities and occupation with your purpose, you have more joy and you activate your highest version.

"Musicians must make music, artists must paint, poets must write if they are ultimately to be at peace with themselves. What humans can be, they must be."

—Abraham Maslow

I personally do not use 'You must' with my clients, but there is great truth in what Abraham Maslow talks about being at peace with yourself, by doing what you were created to do.

Living someone else's design

In an orchestra, there are different categories of musical instruments- percussion, woodwinds, brass, and strings that require different calibers of expertise, style, personality, and pace. If the Cellist tried to play like the violinist, if the Orchestra director played the drums, or if the harpist wanted to play as loud as the tuba player, the performance would fall apart. And that is what happens when we try to live our life following another's purpose. Comparing your sound and volume to others' and playing to their success metrics would result in discontentment and disaster.

Einstein said, "Everybody is a genius. But if you judge a fish by its ability to climb a tree, it will live its whole life believing that it is stupid"

You have a combination of talents, skills, personality and purpose that is unique to you. If you try to pursue others' Key Life Success Indicators and live others' purpose instead of doing what you were put on earth to do, you will always feel empty, regardless of your achievement and accomplishment.

> Unfortunately, life does not come with an Owner's Manual and one's life purpose may not always be so obvious.

So how do you uncover your purpose?

Unfortunately, life does not come with an owner's manual and one's life purpose may not always be so obvious. Your life purpose may be revealed to you in your childhood, or it may take a lifetime. Some knew their purpose when they were kids like Mozart or Stevie Wonder while others, are still seeking in their forties, like I was.

I resigned from my full-time engineering job when my son was two months old because I just wanted to be a full-time mother to my children. Along the way, I started a part-time entrepreneurial journey, which helped me tap deeper into my potential and generate an income. I pursued an MBA and that helped further in building my competence and I started working as a free-lance consultant, that gave me time and flexibility I desired as a mother. During my first marriage, I was not allowed to wholly express my creative right brain, and that still left me with the dissatisfaction of not being my best self. But once my ex-husband and I agreed to separate, I started to explore my creative passions, art, acting, performing, and hosting.

I surprised myself in many ways, e.g., I had never really painted before I was 33 and now my paintings are displayed in galleries. I bloomed in a way that even people unaware of my personal life noticed the transformation.

It was only when I discovered my purpose and started walking in it that I was able to operate from a space of bliss, ease, inspiration, and abundance.

My journey took to me acting in feature films and performing on stages. I was dubbed the Adrenaline Junkie in the leading newspaper in Kampala. I enjoyed the premiers and limelight and adventures, but I came to realize that that fame did not fill the gaps within my soul. It was only when I discovered my purpose and started walking in it that I was able to operate from a space of bliss, ease, inspiration, and abundance. And the more I started living my purpose, I started seeing new, surprising opportunities unfold. So, how do you find out your calling?

Steps to uncover your purpose
Your purpose is a treasure that only you can unearth. In some cases, it may be difficult to pinpoint or fully understand the purpose of your life. Just remember that no coach, book, guru, or seminar can tell you what you were created for. But, the system in this chapter will help you start this exciting and beautiful adventure of uncovering your purpose. I would strongly recommend setting aside ample undistracted time for this chapter.

Your identity and belief systems uncovered in the previous chapters are a foundation on which your purpose is built. Answering life-defining questions like, "Who am I?" and "What do I really believe in?" should have helped you get closer in your path of self-discovery.

If you have not completed the exercise and filled out the first part of the Manifesto, please go back and do it. The activities in the following sections will build on what you uncovered to help raise your awareness and dig deep to help you pick up any patterns or themes that your life has been following. The summation of your experiences, strengths, personality and the impact you have had so far acts as a compass to direct you towards your calling.

We will use the My Life Purpose Worksheet on Page 88 for this exercise. I suggest using the other note sheets available in the book as you may need more space. Also, use a pencil for this exercise as there will be a lot of writing and re-writing. Be true to yourself and be patient. As you go through the sections, something may strike a chord and your life purpose may be revealed to you just like that. On the other hand, you may still feel lost and confused. That is ok. At the end of the chapter, we will talk about it. Even if you don't get total clarity about your life purpose from this chapter, you will get closer to understanding what you were put on this earth for. The following sections will help you find clues to your life purpose.

> It is your responsibility to bring your strengths to life and the activity in this section will help you uncover your strengths.

STEP 1- Strengths:

To understand your purpose, you need to increase awareness of your strengths, which are primarily a combination of your talents, skills, and passions. It is your responsibility to bring your strengths to life and the activity in this section will help you uncover your strengths.

a. Talents/gifts:

A talent is a natural ability or skill that you possess. Each person has endowments that they have probably inherited, but most often people go through life without realizing them because they don't see it. You are so used to it that you don't recognize that what you do with ease does not flow easily for others.

Ponder quietly for five minutes, focusing on one question at a time as you try to recollect your life experiences starting with your childhood memories:

- What are some of the things you are naturally good at? What seems effortless to you?
- Do you remember what came easily to you as a child, maybe something you received recognition for?
- What are the areas where others wished they could do it as well as you?
- What gifts have you identified from books, aptitude tests, or other sources?

Ask your parents for their recollections of your early childhood too, if possible. Move forward into memories from your youth.

Looking back at my life, even though I was a responsible teenager, I was quite purposeless and lived life negotiating at the minimum. However, though I did not put my focus on excelling in academics in my engineering college, I was popular, friendly, compassionate and supportive of the underdog. Two things that stand out are that I was part of the leadership in the college student body and very comfortable performing on stage. I did not connect those experiences to my career at all and for a long time, I considered it a thing of the past. After hiding behind computers for a long time, I started speaking and performing. I delivered a TEDx Talk and have spoken on several stages. Consecutively, I acquired a Life Coaching and Train the Trainer certification to help me develop my capacity further.

Such life experiences in childhood and teenage years can reveal your natural abilities. Summarise your answer in the Talents Section of the worksheet. Circle those that are most unique.

DO IT NOW Once you have identified your talents, see how much you are
utilizing right now.

Some people go through life burying their talents, even if they are aware of them. It is up to you to activate your talents and gifts and bring them to life as your purpose is always in alignment with them.

b. Passions:
Your passions are things or activities that you absolutely love and that drive you. Engaging in such will energize you and make your heart smile. It will fill you with joy, which is beyond happiness; it is a deeper sense of pleasure and comfort, irrespective of external circumstances. Understanding your passions can give you clues towards your purpose.

T. D. Jakes said, "If you can't figure out your purpose, figure out your passion. For your passion will lead you right into your purpose"

Here are some questions you can ask yourself to help you identify your passions
- What makes you experience indescribable joy from within?
- What were some of your childhood pleasures – activities, places, experiences, traditions, food, etc.?

- What activities or causes make you feel alive, inspire you and bring meaning to your life.
- What gives you boundless energy?
- What activities do you get lost in?
- What are your hobbies or interests?

Once you have identified your passions, write them down in the Passions Section of the Worksheet.

When you identify, follow and fuel your passions and joys, you experience a deeper connection to your true self and your purpose in the world. Your passions may seem all over the place and maybe inward-focused, but the magic happens, when you align your passions with your higher calling. The most fulfilled people in the world and put time and effort into igniting their passions.

> **QUICK TIP** Pick the top five and see how you can engage in your passions on a regular basis. Cutting down ten minutes of social media usage daily can free up seventy minutes in a week. That is plenty of time to sing, paint, volunteer, or learn a new skill.

c. Skills:

Skills are a combination of your knowledge, competencies, and the abilities you have learned or acquired through life and work experiences. The skills you have gained on your journey are a major part of your strengths and may give you valuable direct or indirect hints towards uncovering your purpose.

Think about this:
- What are you skilled at?
- What are some of your unique skills?
- What was your education or training focused on?
- What are new fields you are learning about?
- What new skills are you learning?

These questions should be pretty straightforward, unlike talents and passions that need some deep diving. Write down your top skills in the Skills section of the Worksheet.

Note: Some skills may not seem relevant to you, but they may still have an indirect impact on your purpose.

For example, even though I did not pursue a career in engineering, I still apply what I learned in the four years of college to my work and life. The course has helped build my systematic and analytic skills and has given me an edge in navigating and simplifying complex problems to get a solution. Learning is never wasted.

So, now that you have listed your Talents, Passions, and Skills you should be able to have a better understanding of your Strengths. Remember you will be more productive and fulfilled when you take time developing and optimizing your strengths than fixing your weaknesses. When you find ways to optimally align your strengths with your day-to-day activities, you become limitless.

> Remember you will be more productive and fulfilled when you take time developing and optimizing your strengths than fixing your weaknesses.

If your life is completely misaligned with your strengths, you don't always have to just jump up and take a different direction. You can make time to exercise, build and tone your strengths over the weekends while continuing what you need to do. I remember designing pots over the weekends while I worked in a full-time job. It gave me such an escape from the rigidity of the 9-5 job and energized me to push through the following week.

Sometimes you may not be sure of your strengths and interests. For most of my life, I thought I loved ballet and craved for an opportunity to learn that art, but when I finally got a chance to learn it, I did not enjoy it as much. That is ok. The best way to know if you enjoy something is by trying it out and there is no shame in changing directions. Discovering your potential and maximizing it is a continual process that creates a pathway towards your purpose.

STEP 2- Life experiences:
a. Childhood Thoughts and Dreams
Reflect on your thoughts and dreams as a child, before life got complicated. What did you want to become when you grew up? Even if it was something you consider absurd, like being a ninja, or superhero, don't dismiss it. It may hold some valuable clues.

As a child, one of the things I wanted to become was an actress, which would be considered a delusional thought at that time. In India, the average person loves Bollywood movies and idolizes the actors, but God-forbid, a middle-class girl like me talked about becoming an actress. You would be lectured of all the evils in the film industry. I had long forgotten about those dreams but subconsciously carried them on. As an adult, the interest in films was reignited and at the age of thirty-six, I acted in a lead role in my first feature film, The Ugandan.

Write down any thoughts or dreams that stand out from your childhood into the Childhood Thoughts & Dreams Section of the Worksheet and see If you can find any theme or surprising hints towards your purpose.

b. Pains/ Life Changing Events/ Failures

Think about failures, obstacles you have faced, adversities you have overcome or life-changing events in your life. Such difficult experiences teach us powerful life lessons that we would never be able to learn otherwise. As much as it may be hard to hear, good can come out of the worst of situations. We undergo paradigm shifts in our mindset and grow in character and strength. There is no such thing as wasted pain or experience. My painful marriage taught me to stop judging and empathize better, losing our first baby taught me to deal with pain better, falling on stage in the middle of a beauty pageant taught me that life may knock you down, but I had to take responsibility to stand up. Now as a coach and trainer, I have been able to and coach several women going through painful situations.

Write down the theme of such experiences in the Pains Section of the worksheet and think of who can benefit from what you learned.

c. Synchronicity

Synchronicity is a concept first introduced by analytical psychologist Carl Jung, to describe circumstances that appear meaningfully related but lack a causal connection. Also referred to as coincidences, they are unrelated events that align in unexplainable and surprising ways beyond what can be rationalized. These events can form some meaning and guide your purpose. If you think back upon your life, you may recollect seeing a signpost or bumper sticker

82

saying what you needed to hear, getting a call from a friend you just thought of, or maybe something relating to your emotional state may have just been mentioned in a movie you were watching.

I could share numerous synchronicities in my life, that somehow connected beautifully with what was happening in my inner world. I personally do not believe in coincidences but see them as God's way of connecting with us and meeting us at our point of need. I recall a wonderful incident that touched me deep down in my heart. One of the unpleasant memories in my first marriage was my birthdays. Having come from a family where birthdays were made a big deal about, being in a marriage where they were not celebrated, left me feeling alone, sad, and insignificant on those days. But I remember one such sad birthday morning. As I was pulling out of my driveway to go to work, the most beautiful blue hummingbird came and tapped at my side mirror. It filled my heart with joy. That encounter with the hummingbird was like a reminder from God that I was not alone, and He was with me. I felt this indescribable conviction that through all the trials, He was watching over me. I share more about this in Chapter 12.

Synchronicities can hold clues to your ultimate purpose in life, and such experiences can result in a conviction that you are on the right path or that you have made the right choice.

You may have your own beliefs and philosophy and you can have your own interpretation that works for you. Regardless, synchronicities can hold clues to your ultimate purpose in life, and such experiences can result in a conviction that you are on the right path or that you have made the right choice. As you pay closer attention to life around you, you will begin to notice and experience more of these tiny wonders in life. Make note of any such occurrences that had any influence on your life in the Synchronicities Section of the worksheet.

Reflect on your life and think of all the sub-sections in STEP 2 of the worksheet and see if there is a pattern emerging towards your purpose.

STEP 3- Personality:
Your personality is your characteristic way of thinking, feeling and behaving that makes you unique. It influences different areas of your life and so, understanding your personality can help you get some clarity on your purpose.

There are many personality assessments available online that can help you identify your personality type. I would recommend a personality assessment test created by psychologists called The Myers-Briggs Type Inventory (MBTI). There are free versions available. Once you get the results of a Personality test, think through the questions below:

- What aspect of your personality do you love the most?
- What are some aspects of your personality that you love?
- How well do you work with others?
- How best do you express yourself?
- Who are you most comfortable communicating with?

Your purpose
is always
bigger than
you and
beyond your
domain.

In the My Life Purpose Worksheet, write down a few words best describing your personality in the Personality Section.

STEP 4- Impact:

Your purpose is always bigger than you and beyond your domain. You were not given gifts and talents to grow and prosper within your personal space. You are called to improve the life of others- your family, your society, your country, and maybe the world.

"We were placed on earth to fulfill a purpose, and that purpose is what gives meaning to our lives, you ascend to the world to make an impact and make a difference." Myles Munroe

Think along these lines:

- What difference are you making on another human being?
- Whom are you impacting?
- How can you make a difference beyond your world?

Enter your thoughts into the Impact Section of the Worksheet.

STEP 5- Your ideal world:

If the world was an ideal place, how would it look like to you? How are people interacting with each other? How do you feel?
Write it down in the My Ideal World Section the Worksheet.

STEP 6- Tying it all together:

Look through all that you have written in the worksheet. Think through it and see if you can discover any trajectory that your life has been taking. The sections in the Worksheet throw light into some layers buried deep within. So, take time to reflect on them.

Now is the time to tie all the above together to form a draft Purpose statement as shows in Step 5 of the Worksheet.

Other questions that can guide you are:
- What problem have you solved in the past?
- What solutions are you offering right now?
- What problem do you think you were created to solve?
- Whose problems are you solving?

Reflecting on these will help you build the draft statement of your Life Purpose. Like I said earlier, this is not a system to 'download' your life's purpose. The above sections provide you an inventory of clues that will help you see connections to the things you were meant to do in your life.

STEP 7- Final Purpose Statement:

Cross-check your purpose statement with your identity, values, and beliefs that you entered in your Manifesto, recraft your final Purpose Statement and write it down in the Worksheet. Review and revise your Statement as needed

MANIFESTO Enter your Life Purpose Statement into your Personal Manifesto under "My Life Purpose is..." on Page 135.

Does a purpose change over time?

Think about the parts of the body. The purpose of the kidney is to remove waste and extra fluids from the body, and they play a major role in maintaining equilibrium in the body system. The kidney cannot start trying to do the work of the liver.

You were put on earth to do something specific. You have a unique design for that purpose, and nobody can do what you are supposed to do as well as you do it. Your purpose evolves even as you evolve as a person, but it will not change to something drastically different. On this journey of self-discovery and uncovering your purpose, you can live your purpose in several ways. But when you look back over the years, you will notice that your life heads towards one purpose. They can narrow or widen in focus, as we go through different life experiences and milestones.

Referring to the example of the scientific calculator, it was designed with a lot of thought and precision for computing complex operations. It can be used as a paperweight, but that is not its 'why?" The same

"It's not enough to have lived. We should be determined to live for something." —Winston S. Churchill

applies to you. You can revisit, renew and refine your sense of purpose, but your 'why?" will not change.

If the purpose is still not clear
The worksheet is a good starting point for you to create a purpose statement. The statement is your own, so it cannot be very far from the truth, even if you feel that it is not exactly your purpose. Open your mind and spirit and repeat and enjoy the process one step at a time and you will keep getting more clues on the journey. Eventually, you will be able to narrow it down to a strategic life mission.
Take some time to quieten your mind. Say this purpose statement out loud, even if it is not clear or fancy. Own it. Declare it and release it. As you do that, you will feel a connection with yourself at a deeper level and see new truths unfold.

Find purpose in what you are doing today
If you are still confused, don't be disheartened. Seeking your purpose and actively finding purpose in what you do in your daily life will take you closer to the truth. Whether it is being a parent, professional, or a homemaker, make it your purpose to be the best there is and take deliberate steps to share your gifts with others. Your purpose will unfold at the right time if you allow it to.

> Seeking your purpose and actively finding purpose in what you do in your daily life will take you closer to the truth.

Conclusion
There is a great story that I read somewhere.
A farmer found an eagle's egg and decided to put it along with the other eggs in the hen's coop. The eagle hatched and grew among the hens knowing that it was a chicken.
One day when he looked up, he saw this magnificent creature flying up in the sky. When he asked around, he learned that it was an eagle, the king of the sky. But he was told, "Don't waste your time looking up there, you are a chicken", "Stay within your limits, you are

a chicken." And this eagle continued his life as a chicken. Deep inside he knew something was missing, but since he was continuously told that he was a chicken he suppressed his unexplained dreams and thoughts.

But one day, when he could not hold it in any longer, he decided to try to fly. He went to the highest spot, and spread his wing, and plunged, he flapped a little but fell. His wings had not developed enough. But he did not give up. He was opposed for his 'foolishness' and laughed at, but he kept trying. Eventually, he was able to fly and one fine day, he took off soaring into the sky.

I have an addition to that story. One of the chickens watching felt like he was short-changed and decided that he should fly too. He kept trying but never succeeded. People told him, "keep trying, one day you will succeed". His failed attempts led to frustration and resentment. He stopped being grateful for the food, shelter, and protection that was provided to him. Instead, he spent the rest of his life in bitterness and regrets.

Are you an eagle living a chicken's life? Are you pecking on the ground when you have wings that were meant to soar? Or, maybe you're feeling like a failure because you don't have wings like an eagle and instead of being grateful for the gifts, opportunities, family, security, and peace you have, you spend your life pitying yourself?

"If you can tune into your purpose and really align with it, setting goals so that your vision is an expression of that purpose, then life flows much more easily." — Jack Canfield

It's time for you to take responsibility for your life and what you have been designed for. Understand what the Creator's purpose for your life is and own it. Don't limit yourself trying to be somebody else. Instead, strive to be the best version of you.

Living a life of purpose can bring an aspect of fulfillment to virtually everything you do. When you acknowledge your purpose and live life by your design, abundance will flow - an abundance of peace, health, fulfillment, joy, provision and you will lead a satisfying and meaningful life.

My Life Purpose Worksheet

My Success Metrics

STEP 1:

TALENTS:

PASSIONS:

SKILLS:

STRENGTHS-
Talents/ Skills/ Passions

- Write down all your Talents. Circle those that are unique to you
- Write down your skills. Circle those that are unique to you
- Write down your Passions/interests. Circle those that are unique to you

STEP 2:

CHILDHOOD THOUGHTS & DREAMS:

PAINS:

SYNCHRONICITIES:

LIFE EXPERIENCES

Write down your life experiences:
- Childhood Thoughts & Dreams:
- Life-changing Events/ Adversities/ Challenges you have overcome
- Synchronicities

Any direction you feel your life is going in?

STEP 3:

PERSONALITY

PERSONALITY

What would best describe your Personality? How do you best express yourself?

STEP 4:

IMPACT

IMPACT

What difference are you making on another human being? Whom are you impacting?

STEP 5:

YOUR IDEAL WORLD:

YOUR IDEAL WORLD

If the world was an ideal place, how would it look to you?

STEP 6:

My purpose is to use my(Pick two from 1) _____
and_____ to help(if any particular group
stands out from 2 or 4)_____ to
create(from 3&5) _____
_____
_____

DRAFT PURPOSE STATEMENT

Use the clues above to write a draft purpose statement. This can be a starting point.

STEP 7:

My Purpose is to :

REVIEW AND WRITE
THE FINAL PURPOSE STATMENT

- Cross-check the statement with your Manifesto.
- Revise it if needed and recraft your final Life Purpose Statement

11

Your True Desires

Now that you have a better understanding of who you are (identity), where you are (belief system) and why you are here (purpose), you can better answer the question, "What do I really desire?". Answering this question in all honesty will help you set Key Life Success Indicators (KLSIs) that are true to you, ones that will bring meaning and gratification into your life.

In one of my business groups, a lady was venting about how she was struggling in her online business. She was disappointed with the lack of human connection she felt in the virtual space and did not feel the online model of her business was suiting her. Most people were encouraging her to keep trying, pushing and hustling. That is what people generally tell you if are struggling to progress towards your goals- "Keep striving", "Fight or die trying!", "Never say never!". So, you keep striving in the same direction because everyone is doing it or because everyone is telling you to do it. You do not pause to ask yourself if that is what you really want. After all the hustle and bustle, even if you do not burn out and successfully manage to achieve all you set out to, you don't experience happiness and fulfillment. Why? It's because the things you pursued were not what you desired; you were chasing someone else's dream.

In the last chapters of this section, we learned that we are all unique and what you want may be different than what the other person wants. The truth is, many times, what you think you want is not what you really want. This chapter builds on the previous chapters in trying to chip away parts of you that are not in alignment with who you truly are and what you truly want. Living your life based on what others think is best for you, or to impress others or to avoid being rejected, is giving away your power to create your own happiness.

Limiting beliefs
In Chapter 7, we debunked some beliefs that could hold you back from living your best version. As a child, you were clear about what you wanted and made no pretense about it. Then through early

childhood programming drills, you were told what is bad, good, what you should do and what you should not. Suggestions like, "Don't ask what you want, you look greedy", "Don't dream too big" and such suggestions may have numbed your true desires. Some other common debilitating phrases you may have heard growing up:

- "You can't have it all"
- "The higher you go the harder you fall"
- "What you want is not important as long as everybody around you is happy"
- "You always ask too much"
- "Stay within your limits" *"Apni aukaat main reh" is a common Hindi phrase.*
- "You can't get_____ because you are not_____"

Such beliefs influence your perception of what you truly want and the KLSIs that you set for yourself.

Write down beliefs/excuses you recognize that have warped your sense of what you want to do, who you want to be, where you want to go, and other things you want?

How can you reframe these beliefs to empower you to take a step towards going for what you really want?

Social influences

In addition to your limiting beliefs, you are constantly bombarded by suggestions around you that latch on to your subconscious mind and cloud your judgment of what you desire as a person.

Companies spend hundreds of billions of dollars annually on advertisements with the sole objective of convincing you that you need their product or services. You have heard the saying, "A good salesman can sell a refrigerator to the Eskimos". I do not know much about Eskimos and whether they use refrigerators, but this statement was referring to the skill of selling something that the person does not need. The "Torches of Freedom" is a classic example, where women were encouraged to smoke. Smoking was promoted as a symbol of emancipation and equality with men. This marketing strategy 'opened a gold mine right in their backyard' as quoted by the President of the company and the women fell for it. I have nothing against smoking, other than it being hazardous to health, but I wonder if the women were really aware of what they wanted and if they knew how they had fallen prey to some corporation's strategy to increase their bottom line.

Many companies even use psychology tools to see how they can manipulate you into desiring what they want you to. Their promotional tools and algorithms plant ideas about the ideal lifestyle, body size, what your clothes or house should look like, and overall, what success looks like. In this age of digitalization, you cannot hide from constant subconscious messages on every device you hold. Such message can influence the Success Metrics you have set for yourself at a subliminal level. They condition you to want more.

Add to this, the pressure of keeping up with the Joneses and the fear of missing out (FOMO) and you lose yourself in the mix and internally focus on being better than the next person. The comparison game is one you will never win because there will always be somebody with a better house, a better resume, or a better body. Ultimately, your real wants and desires get buried deeper under these pretentious layers.

Take a minute to consider where your desires stem from? Understanding what fuels your desire will help you block out suggestions that do not serve you and peel away desires that are not true to you. It will help you define what you really want, what is right for you and what works for you.

Understanding what fuels your desire will help you block out suggestions that do not serve you and peel away desires that are not true to you.

Not everything good is right
There are many things you want that may be good, but they may not necessarily be right for you. They may be right for you, but they may not be the right thing for you at this time. We go chasing several 'good' things and end up losing focus on things that are most important to us. I know many who gave up their jobs to volunteer because it was a 'good' thing and ended up neglecting their family. There are people all around who follow every shiny offer and shop for the best deals and end up in debt and with things they don't need.

All those are good things, but you need to examine if they are really in line with who you are, your purpose, and what you want. Even if it is the right thing, it is important to ask, "Is it what I want right now?", "Is it taking me away from area of focus at this time?", "Is it compromising other areas of my life?"

I can give an example about how I was chasing 'good' stuff that was not necessarily right for me. I call myself a learning junkie. I get that from my Dad who is still taking music lessons in his 70s. I bought about hundred hours' worth of increadible courses in 2020 in the period during the pandemic COVID-19. I loved gaining all the new information. I immersed myself in those courses for endless hours and before I knew it, I was compromising on my health and family responsibilities. I had to remind myself that not everything good is right for me and not everything good is right for me every time. So, understanding that you don't have to want every good thing, helps you to better define what you want. And that will prevent you from being swayed in different directions by every good thing.

So, understanding that you don't have to want every good thing, helps you to better define what you want.

I just want to be happy

I hear many clients say, "I just want to be happy". But defining happiness is not easy as it can mean many different things to different people. Many people have reached dead ends in the quest for happiness.

In positive psychology, there are two popular approaches to happiness- hedonic and eudaemonic. Hedonic happiness focuses on experiences of pleasure and enjoyment, while eudaemonic happiness is achieved through experiences of meaning, self-realization, and purpose. Both contribute to your overall well-being in different ways, but, as much as attaining hedonic pursuits may give you instant gratification, the novelty wears off eventually. So, when you are setting your Key Life Success Indicators, it is important to have a healthy balance of metrics that bring hedonic and eudaemonic happiness.

So how do you know your true desires?

This section will help you clarify what you truly want. Once you are clear about your true desires, your journey towards attaining them will be as joyful and meaningful as attaining them.

Let's get started. We will work on the My Desires Worksheet on Page 97. Use a pencil for this activity as there will a lot of draft work. If you need more space, use the notes sheets available in the book.

STEP 1- What are you pursuing right now?
List down the major things that you are pursuing right now that are taking your resources in the first column in PART 1 –purchases, home projects, courses, hobbies, relationships, vacations, etc.

STEP 2- Why are you doing it?
Are you doing it because you should, or because you want to? Are you doing it because of someone else? Is your decision to do it influenced primarily by social media, society, friends, or upbringing? Are you seeking validation from it? Are you hoping for it to complete you? Enter your reasons in the second column of PART I.

> The fear of being judged, criticized, or rejected by people who don't care about you, should not be a motivation for you to keep doing something you don't want.

STEP 3- Things you don't want.
Having read about the subtle influences on your desires, ask yourself if you really want the things you have listed. Is there anything there that you don't want to do? There may be cases where you may need to engage in things you don't want to, as part of the process of reaching your long-term goals. However, if you don't have a good reason to pursue things you do not want, strike them out. The fear of being judged, criticized, or rejected by people who don't care about you, should not be a motivation for you to keep doing something you don't want. You will save your time, energy, focus, and heart by focusing on things you want to do.

If your intention is to please people, remember it's not possible, they will always find some shortcomings. And the drudgery of doing things you really don't want, can result in an inner conflict that will affect your well-being.

"Be who you are and say what you feel, because those who mind don't matter and those who matter don't mind." Dr. Seuss

If you are doing undesirable things short-term, for people who matter in your life, it may be worth the ride. Again, it is for you to think closely and assess your gain and what you stand to lose. Enter your responses in the third column of PART I. Strike off items as needed.

STEP 4- What do you want that you are not pursuing right now?
Think of the things you want in life that you have been putting aside. This is between you and only you, so open up and be true to yourself. Are there dreams you have buried because they seemed unattainable? You are your own limitation. Dismiss voices that tell you that you are too small, too old, not worthy, too insignificant, or not enough. Don't settle for the minimum. What do you want for your family, career, health, relationships, etc.? Whom do you want to help? What possessions do you want to acquire? What places do you want to see? How much money do you want to make? What skills would you like to acquire? What is your soul whispering to you to do, have, or be?
Write them down in the first column of PART II in the worksheet.

"The only thing that's keeping you from getting what you want is the story you keep telling yourself." Tony Robbins.

STEP 5- Question the motive behind your desire:
Ask yourself, why you want it? And keep asking "WHY?" till you get the final answer and write it down in the second column of PART II in the worksheet.

Asking this question will allow your true desires to emerge. If you discover that the reason you want something, is to prove a point, impress others, get back at someone or validate yourself, then you need to reframe your mindset or adjust your dreams as needed. If you have a solid motivation to achieve something, the chances of achieving them are higher.

STEP 6- Is this me?
Ask yourself whether you would want this even if nobody was watching and regardless of what others have? Answer this question in the third column of PART II for each item you have listed and cross out items that do not align with who you truly are.

"We buy things we don't need with money we don't have to impress people we don't like." Dave Ramsey

Many times, we pursue things for the sake of status or to keep up with others. Such pursuits can take away your focus and resources from things you really desire.

STEP 7- Cross-check with your Manifesto:
Refer to your manifesto now. Reflect on who you really are, your values, and your purpose, and see if the remaining desires on the list in PART I and PART II are in alignment with your authentic self. Feel free to change, edit, strike off items on the list to uncover your authentic desires.

MANIFESTO Recraft these desires into statements with powerful action verbs and write them into your Personal Manifesto on Page 135, under "I want to.."

Examples of desire statements for the Manifesto:
I want to be the best husband/wife/ father/ mother.
I want to expand my horizons in terms of my business.
I want to make money doing what I love.
I want to get to the top of my career.
I want to be happier, healthier and more energized.
I want to 'be' more, live more, and create more.
I want to play a part in changing people's lives and leave a legacy.
I want to be a good steward of the gifts given to me.

"Clarity is power. The more clear you are about what you want the more likely you are to achieve it." -Billy Cox

Conclusion
If you do not know what you want, others will decide it for you. Knowing what you want in a way that is authentic to you will help you stay focused on your journey. You will be empowered to take back your power and say no to people and activities that do not align with what you want and to stand your ground in the face of adversities. Most of all, knowing that you are pursuing what is authentic to your wants will keep you excited through the journey.
Now that you have received better clarity of what you truly want, you are ready to redefine what success means to you and to formulate your personal KLSIs in the next section of this book.

As I conclude this section of the book, I want to share an Indian story, The 99 Club, that has been going around the internet for years. I do not have the source, but this is in line with what we learned in this chapter about having clarity of what we want.

The 99 Club

There once lived a King who, despite a life filled with luxuries, was neither happy nor content. One day, the King came upon a common peasant who was singing happily while he worked. The happiness of a common man fascinated the King. He questioned why the ruler of the land with all the luxuries was unhappy and gloomy, while a poor peasant had so much joy in his life? The King asked the man, "Why are you so happy?"

"Your Majesty, I am a common man, but my family and I don't need much, just warm food to fill us and a roof over our heads," the man answered

The king was not satisfied with the man's answer so, later in the day, he sought advice from one of his most trusted advisers. After listening to the King the adviser said, "Your Majesty, I believe that the man, you saw, has not yet been made part of The 99 Club."

"The 99 Club? What is that?" inquired the King.

The adviser replied, "Your Majesty, to understand The 99 Club you must first place 99 Gold coins in a bag and leave it on the man's doorstep." And so the king did what the adviser told him to do.

After a tiring day working in the fields, the man was returning to his house when he saw a bag on his doorstep. He took the bag into his house and opened it. He let out a great shout of joy when he discovered that the bag was filled with gold coins.

He began to count all the gold coins. After several counts, he was convinced that there were only 99 coins. He wondered, "What could've happened to that last gold coin? No one would leave just 99 coins!"

So he looked everywhere he could, but he did not find the 100th coin. After a while, he was exhausted and decided that he was going to work harder than ever to earn that gold coin and complete his collection with the 100th coin.

From that day, the man's life was changed. He overworked and turned horribly grumpy. He castigated his family for not helping him to achieve his goal of earning the 100th gold coin. He stopped singing while he worked and only thought about getting the 100th coin to complete his collection.

The King witnessed the drastic transformation in the man and was puzzled. The king asked the advisor why the man wasn't happy and satisfied anymore. The adviser replied, "Your Majesty, the man is now a member of The 99 Club."

He continued, "The 99 Club contains those people who have enough to be happy, but are not content, because they're always striving for that one extra thing, telling themselves: "I will be happy if I get that one final thing in my life."

My Success Metrics My Desires Worksheet

Part I

WHAT AM I PURSUING RIGHT NOW?	WHY AM I PURSUING IT?	DO I REALLY WANT IT?

Part II

WHAT DO I WANT THAT I AM NOT PURSUING RIGHT NOW?	WHY DO I WANT IT?	IS IT REALLY ME?

NOTES

12

Your Inner Power

There are many things in life that we cannot explain – unexpected things happen, and we have questions that don't have straight answers. At times as such, when things are beyond my understanding, I have found strength in tapping into a Higher Power within me. I have written this based on my belief in God. You can call Him a Cosmic Force, Owner of the Universe, Intuitive Knowing, Instinct, Inner Voice, whatever you like, but if this goes against your belief you can skip to the next chapter without affecting your journey of redefining your Success Metrics. I just share my experience when I was in a dark place of how God turned my sorrow into joy and helped me discover who I was and my purpose in life. You are free to have your own philosophies and beliefs if they work for you.

I want to explicitly state that I am in no way promoting any religion, doctrine, or a religious man; my faith is based on a relationship with God as our Creator and Father. I refer to the Bible and Jesus, but they are universally accessible to all and are not restricted to a particular religion as you may have been led to believe. I am not a proponent of religion. I do not mean to offend any religion or religious person. I respect you and I love you in all sincerity; I am only sharing my experience with religion here.

I was raised in a religious home with strong Christian values and I was a firm religious Christian. In my first marriage, even when I was utterly broken inside, I held on to the marriage because religion taught me that was the right thing to do. When I turned to the religious leaders in tears seeking intervention, they urged me to ignore, compromise, and adjust in the marriage. They judged me based on the rules that religion had set. I realized they cared more about protecting the religion than they did about me. At many points of hopelessness, I prayed for death as that felt better than the anguish I endured in the marriage. That is when I started questioning all I had believed. How can religion cause someone to choose death over life? How could any God as a Father, encourage His child to live in a space of endless pain? As I started questioning the Creator himself, I started seeing things differently. He assured me that I was precious to him. That gave me hope to live. Religion had convinced me that God cared more about the religious doctrines than he cared about my happiness, well-being, and my dreams. But I was wrong. He cares for us. It was when I started separating God from religion, that I really understood His heart and realized how religion could potentially misrepresent God. I now see God as a Father, who loves us unconditionally and wants the best for us.

We are spiritual beings
We are spiritual beings and are consciously or subconsciously on an inner journey of seeking answers to life's mysteries and a connection with God. So, ignoring this aspect of your being may result in a lack of meaning in your life. Note that spirituality is not about renouncing your material possessions and living a secluded life on a mountain. It is not about satisfying your individual needs at all, whether spiritual or self-actualization. We are not designed for isolation but connection- connection to God as a Father and to each other as His children.

You are His workmanship created with a unique combination of talents, skills, passions, personality for a purpose that only you can fulfill.

He created us.
Our body is made up of eleven systems intricately working with each other to help us breathe, walk, talk, sing, laugh, love, and empathize. I don't know if the rumors of Charles Darwin withdrawing his Evolution Theory are true or not, but nobody can convince me that we evolved from fish. God created you wonderfully, fearfully, and lovingly. You are not an accident and are precious in His sight.

He has a purpose for you.
If you still have questions about your true identity, beliefs, and purpose, why not ask the One who created you what he placed you on Earth for? You are His workmanship created with a unique combination of talents, skills, passions, personality for a purpose that only you can fulfill.

He wants to bless us
Religion made me feel that God did not want us to enjoy life and was withholding good things from us. I had restricted my dreams. But God wants to bless us, not just spiritually, but in all ways.

He is accessible at all times

Religion can complicate this. Parents do not set up rules for children to access them but are available for them whenever needed. That is the same with our Father in heaven. Seek and you will find Him. If you have doubts, fears, confusions, or questions, just ask Him. He is omnipresent, meaning He is everywhere. You can talk to Him right now at home, in your office, or in your car. You do not need any device, object, tool, or be in a specific location to speak to Him. Prayer is simply conversing with Him. When things go wrong or you feel alone, just talk to Him, whether loudly or silently in your heart. You don't need fancy language or religious terminologies, just be you.

He speaks to us

As you talk to Him, He will speak to you. You may not always hear His voice, but He speaks through dreams, visions, people, epiphanies, signs, and synchronicities or through a whisper in your soul. Make it a habit to spend some time with Him daily and let Him direct you. The more I allow myself to lean into His plan, His purpose is being fulfilled in and through me. If I pursue a direction that is not right for me, He nudges me onto the right path through ways that may look like coincidences.

His ways are not our ways

God's measure of success is different, as is His timing, and His ways to attain success. His ways are not our ways and His thoughts are not our thoughts. When the world says go faster, He may tell you to take a break or rest. When the world tells you to hold on tight and fight, He may tell you to release. He may even lead you to do something that you are not naturally inclined to do. Many times, the guidance I get from Him defeats logic and reason but falls in place beautifully at the right time. Submitting to Him has given me peace that surpasses understanding, even amid storms.

Conclusion

As you continue having conversations with your Creator you will get more clarity. Surrender your Key Life Success Indicators, dreams, goals and plans to Him and He will guide you. Above all, being aware that someone, who knows what tomorrow looks like, is watching out for you, will give you strength on your journey.

NOTES

My Success Metrics SECTION III

13

Create Your Personal KLSIs

In Section II, you went through the process of understanding and eliminating the blocks that have been holding you back, gaining a better understanding of who you are, your values and what you want, and your purpose. If you have followed all the steps, you have almost completed your Personal Manifesto.

The components in your Personal Manifesto are the building blocks of writing authentic Key Life Success Indicators. In this chapter, we will tie them all together to break free from the social constructs of the generalized 'Success Paths' and create a life you love living.

Your story is in your hands. It is your responsibility to write the next scenes and create an ending that you desire. If you have felt that you have been trapped inside someone else's story, knowingly or unknowingly, willingly or unwillingly, it is time to break free and recreate your story.

I highly recommend you put aside at least one uninterrupted hour for the exercise in this chapter, preferably in a quiet place. You are rewriting your story; you are rewiring your thought patterns and redefining what success means to you. This chapter will give practical steps to create massive shifts in different areas of your life and you need to be patient with this process. If you cannot allocate time to follow the step-by-step guide below, I strongly recommend waiting till you can and committing to revisit this chapter at some point fairly soon. That will help you get the most of this book.

> Your story is in your hands. It is your responsibility to write the next scenes and create an ending that you desire.

Create your KLSIs

We will use the My Key Life Success Indicators Worksheet on Page 110 for the four steps below to create your original KLSIs. This process is a powerfully effective tool for manifesting the best version of your life. In this chapter, we will focus on the long-term KLSIs and in the next chapters, we will reverse-engineer these long-term dreams into short-term KLSIs and goals and break them further into monthly and daily action steps.

The visualization exercise used in this process is based on one of Jack Canfield's Success Principles "See what you want and get what you see". I have used this principle in conjunction with the findings of the previous section that you have compiled into your Manifesto.

STEP 1- Your Personal Manifesto:
Read through the statements in your Personal Manifesto. Declare them out loud, if possible. Close your eyes and experience the peace that flows. Enjoy the liberating feeling that comes with not having to wear masks. Embrace the real you with intentionality, unapologetically.
Now, with your identity, empowering beliefs, values, and purpose in mind for a few minutes, think of how you would like your life to be right now. What do you want to change? How would you like your career, health, relationships, and emotions to be?

STEP 2- Envisioning your overall KLSIs:
The first step in creating the life you want is to have a crystal-clear vision. Envision your life ten, twenty, thirty years from now as relevant. If you could have, be and do anything you wanted, true to yourself, how does life look like to you? How do you feel overall? Are you living a balanced life? Is your behavior different? How is it influencing your overall well-being? Who are the people with you? What are you doing?

The first step in creating the life you want is to have a crystal clear vision.

Our brain does not know the difference between a vividly visualized scene and reality. When you feed your conscious mind with such visualizations, you are tapping into the subconscious mind. The images create a structural tension in the brain, and it looks for ways to release the tension. The process will open up your brain to creative ideas to reach your dreams, you will see shifts in perception, your eyes will be opened to existing opportunities you had never noticed before, and you will see new doors start opening.

Keep referring to your Personal Manifesto so your mind does not wander to what others want for your life, or how you think life 'should' look like. This is your life. You are designing your destiny. If you sense others' thoughts or success metrics taking control of your thoughts, get back in the driver's seat and direct your life back to your personal journey. When you use the visualization techniques in alignment with your authentic self and your purpose, you become unstoppable.

When you use the visualization techniques in alignment with your authentic self and your purpose, you become unstoppable.

STEP 3- Creating KLSIs for each category:

Now that you have the overall vision for your life, envisage your life in different categories. How do you want your life to look like? When you visualize, feel the feeling, place yourself in the future and engage all your senses and emotions. Let go of any limiting beliefs that may come creeping back. Don't confine yourself to the resources you have right now. Don't be pressurized with competing with others. Just keep in mind who you truly are. Let your Manifesto guide you. There is nothing you cannot achieve when you are in alignment with you who are and your purpose. So don't hold back.

"Create the highest, grandest vision possible for your life, because you become what you believe" Oprah Winfrey

Again, do not be tempted to think about how life should be or is supposed to be. Imagine you had no one to answer to, or to impress or please, except yourself and your closest people, how do you see your life in the different categories? Do not impose a limit on your dreams as you go through the process. Read through the categories below and then close your eyes and visualize each category separately. Add as many details as possible to your mental images.

QUICK TIP You can do this exercise for specific durations, like five years or ten years as applicable.

Physical

How is your state of health? Are you feeling strong, full of stamina and vitality? What is your body weight? What activities are you engaged in? Are you seeing yourself jogging/ swimming/ resting or playing full of energy with your grandchildren?

Financial

Are you and your family were well taken for? Are you financially free? Are you going on yearly international vacations? How does your dream house look like? Do you have a good saving scheme? Are you self-sufficient? Do you have multiple income streams? What is your net worth?

Relational

Do you have a life partner? Are you having a blissful, joyful, and intimate relationship with your significant other? Are you having a close bond with your children/ parents? Do you have close, trusting relationships with your friends? Are you spending quality time with the people who are most important to you? What kind of relationship are you having with your co-workers, business associates, subordinates, extended family, etc.? Are you free of all toxic relationships?

Professional

How do you see your career? What is your job title? How is your business doing? Are you growing? What are some of your accomplishments? What major contribution are you making in your career? Are you manifesting your full potential? Are you loving what you do? Are you utilizing and growing your natural talents?

Mental

Do you see yourself mentally alert and active and coherent? Do you feel confident and happy? Do you have a positive attitude? Are you happy and excited about life and the opportunities it presents?

Recreational

Are you having fun? Are you enjoying yourself with your family and friends? Are you having time to relax? Are you learning a new hobby or skill or working on a family project? Are you engaged in any sport?

Spiritual

Are you at peace with your life- present and past? Are you happy with your beliefs and living a full meaningful life? Are you growing in your spiritual walk with your Creator? Is your spiritual journey engendering love and generosity? Do you feel in alignment with yourself, your values, principles, ethics, and morals, and purpose?

Philanthropical

Are you giving back? Are you making a difference in the world in your unique way? Are you making an impact in your community or the world? Are you leaving a legacy? Are you touching lives around you? Some people think you need a lot to be able to give. But each person has something precious to offer.

Now that you are clear about the categories, close your eyes and spend at least 5 mins to visualize each category. Spend 20 – 30 mins going through the whole exercise.

STEP 4- Write it down:

Go to the KLSI worksheet on the next page and write down at least three things in each category. If you want to write more, you can use a journal. Go back to a category and visualize it again if you need.

> QUICK TIP You can customize this exercise to create KLSI's for your family, personal groups or team. You can also add or remove categories as applicable

Viola!!! Congratulations on creating your life's KLSIs. Setting your KLSIs as clearly as possible in a way that is authentic to you, is the first step in achieving them!

When I started doing this process, it filled me with such joy. I hope you feel the same excitement. The path to your dreams may be long or short but knowing that you are headed towards the life that you really want makes the journey extremely thrilling and rewarding.

If you still need clarity, repeat the exercise and refine your KLSIs. Once you have written them down, don't hold on to them tight. Releasing them will give them room to grow and evolve in ways you least expect. But as you go through the process, keep reassessing your KLSIs with your Manifesto regularly. Don't let them unwittingly get away from who you are.

Make a copy of the completed worksheet and put it up at a place you can see daily. Let this be your reference point for the decisions you make on a day-to-day basis. Keeping your eyes on the prize helps you live your life on track and gives you strength and motivation for the journey.

My Key Life Success Indicators

PHYSICAL

FINANCIAL

RELATIONAL

PROFESSIONAL

RECREATIONAL

SPIRITUAL

MENTAL

PHILANTHROPICAL

14

Create Your Success Path

Congratulations!! You now have your personal KLSIs!! You have created a vision for your life in line with your authentic self! The next step is to create a Success Path. Having a vision without goals and action steps, is like knowing where to go, but not having a road map. This chapter will give you 9 Steps that will guide you to create a roadmap to your KLSIs.

STEP 1- Create Your personal Success Path:

A success path is a sequence of activities, tasks, or steps that must be taken to achieve your KSLIs. By mapping out a Success Path for yourself you will have a visual representation of the journey to your KLSIs. The Success Path will include a task sequence, timeline, and calendar, so all you have

> Having a vision without goals and action steps, is like knowing where to go, but not having a road map.

to do is execute. You can break it up into annual, three-year, or ten-year KLSIs to suit your needs. For example, if you are thirty and have a dream of retiring at fifty, you can break your Success Path into two ten-year boxes.

a. Turn to My Success Path Worksheet on Page 116. You can write into this worksheet directly or you can customize this format by dividing the timeline into more or fewer boxes as per your needs and copy it into your journal.
b. Write down your lifetime KLSIs in the last box to the extreme right.
c. Write down your starting point in relation to our end goals in the first box to the extreme left. What is your state of affairs right now?
d. Identify the gaps to get a rough idea of the time and resources needed to fill the gaps.
e. Keeping the KLSIs as your endpoint, work backwards. Think about how you can break up the bigger vision into smaller milestones and enter them into the boxes representing the specific periods starting from the box before the last box. It helps to think through the different options you may have to get from where you are now to where you want to be.

My Success Path For My KLSIs

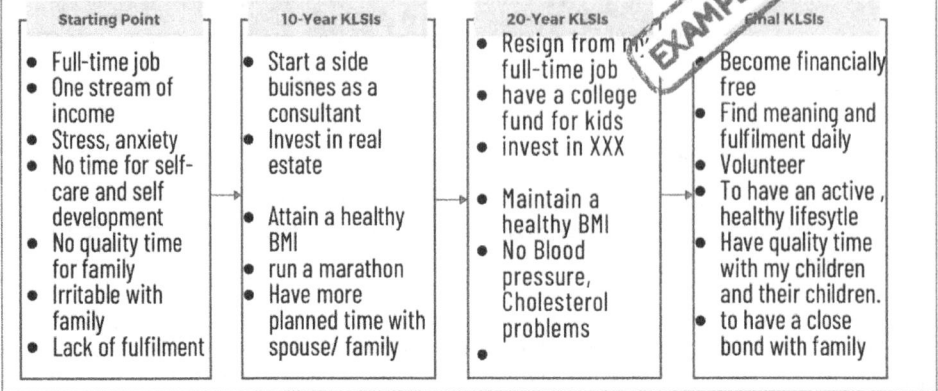

EXAMPLE

Starting Point	10-Year KLSIs	20-Year KLSIs	Final KLSIs
• Full-time job • One stream of income • Stress, anxiety • No time for self-care and self development • No quality time for family • Irritable with family • Lack of fulfilment	• Start a side buisnes as a consultant • Invest in real estate • Attain a healthy BMI • run a marathon • Have more planned time with spouse/ family	• Resign from m'' full-time job • have a college fund for kids • invest in XXX • Maintain a healthy BMI • No Blood pressure, Cholesterol problems •	• Become financially free • Find meaning and fulfilment daily • Volunteer • To have an active , healthy lifesytle • Have quality time with my children and their children. • to have a close bond with family

Here is an example to help you:

As you advance in your journey new opportunities may open up and some things you listed may become irrelevant. Our life's journey is hardly a straight line to the finish. Regardless, this is a good starting point for your Success path.

Having your endpoint in perspective is key in keeping you motivated on the journey. When the going gets tough, many quit because they do not know why they do what they do. Knowing that these KLSIs were not set by someone else but by you personally, will be your greatest motivator.

STEP 2- One-Year KLSIs:

From your timeline in STEP 1, extract your One-Year Key Life Success Indicators. Connecting your long-term KLSIs with your 'today' will increase the certainty of you acting in the 'now' towards reaching your dreams. Also, having yearly KLSIs, help you to assess, rewrite, shift or pivot your next set of KLSIs based on your growth and experience and the new.

Connecting your long-term KLSIs with your 'today' will increase the certainty of you acting in the 'now' towards reaching your dreams.

Turn to Page 117 and write one or two main KLSIs under each Category – Physical, Relational, Professional, Financial, Recreational, Mental, Spiritual and Philanthropical. Think of how your life would need to look one year from now to be able to reach your long-term KLSIs. Remember to keep your Manifesto in perspective as you write the KLSIs.

STEP 3- Write down your goals:

Make 8 copies of the My Goal Success Plan Worksheet on Page 118 for each category of KSLIs. Alternatively, you can just use 8 separate pages in your notebook and jot down the sections.

Starting with one category, write down clear goals that you need to accomplish in the year to reach the One-Year KLSIs. Research has shown that setting goals and writing them, increases the likelihood of reaching the outcome you desire.

Make sure the goals are S.M.A.R.T.

> Research has shown that setting goals and writing them, increases the likelihood of reaching the outcome you desire.

- **SPECIFIC:** Goals like "I want to be happy" and "I want to be healthier" are not specific. What exactly does that mean to you? For example, if you want to increase your income, define what you want your increase to be, what new sources of income you would like to explore, etc. Don't throw random figures. Assess what your abundance metric is. You can keep striving for more but having a figure will give you a sense of achievement and contentment.
- **MEASURABLE:** How will you know you have achieved that goal. E.g., If you say, "I want to have a better attitude", how can you measure it? Some goals are easy to measure like earning X amount or losing X pounds. But you can still think of ways how to measure the abstract goals. E.g., if your KLSI is to have a better relationship with your spouse, you can set goals like putting aside half a day for an outing with your spouse every weekend, having weekly date nights, etc. When you have goals that are measurable, it is easier to achieve it and ascertain your progress.
- **ACHIEVABLE:** "I want to go to the moon," may not achievable right now. Set goals that can challenge you and stretch you, but not break you. You should believe that the goal is achievable.
- **REALISTIC:** You may be able to lose 20 pounds in a month, by not eating, but is that really realistic?
- **TIME-FRAMED:** Each goal you write down must have a deadline, otherwise there is not urgency to complete it. The human brain operates better with time frames.

Formulate your goals to accommodate the S.M.A.R.T system.

Repeat STEP 3 for each category on separate pages.

Examples of SMART Goals:
"I want to be positive", "I want to travel the world", "I want to spend more time with my children" and "I want to declutter the house" are NOT SMART goals
"I want to lose 30 lbs. by March 20XX", "I want the room in the garage to park the cars by Dec 20XX", "I want to be debt-free by June 20XX" and "I want to go on weekly dates with my wife" are SMART Goals.

STEP 4- Create affirmations:
Goal affirmations are positive phrases or statements declaring specific goals as completed.

"If you think you can or if you think you can't, either way, you are right" Henry Ford

There is a fair amount of research behind how affirmations help to combat subconscious patterns and replace them with empowering narratives. We may set great goals, but many times, we self-sabotage through our negative self-talk. There is a part of the brain called the Reticular Activating System (RAS), which is like the command center. If you say things like "I can't do it", "I will surely fail", the RAS will look for ways to making it a reality.

So, fortify your goals with positive affirmations, as statements of faith to create your new reality. Create affirmations in the present tense for each goal you wrote in Step 3 and write them in the worksheet, starting with "I am so happy and grateful that I am now …"

STEP 5 - Visualize your goals:
There is a lot of research done to prove that visualizing desired outcomes, increases the chances of its success.

"Whatever your mind can conceive and believe, you can achieve" Napolean Hill

As explained in the previous chapter, visualizations create a structural tension in our subconscious mind between the desired state and reality. This tension can kick-start a process that guides your decisions towards the desired state. So, for each affirmation, take few minutes to close your eyes and visualize how the outcome will look like, how you feel, how things will be different.

CHECK BLOG Check my blog on the power of visualizations here:
https://www.edlynsabrina.com/post/visualize-your-way-to-success

STEP 6- Chunking:

Now it is time to break down goals into smaller goals or chunks and action steps. For each goal on the copies of Page 118, think of all the smaller steps that will be needed to reach them. Write them down into the My Master Action-List Worksheet on Page 119 as clearly as you possible.

List them down into as many executable tasks as possible and put a deadline against them. This helps in reducing the overwhelm that comes with doing big tasks. Our brain goes into freeze, fight, or flight mode when it is overwhelmed and that causes our logical brain to shut down, thereby allowing the limbic system (the monkey brain) to take charge, leading us to procrastinate.

This helps in reducing the overwhelm that comes with doing big tasks.

Clarifying how you will reach each goal will help give you more confidence, thus helping the brain not to go into 'danger' mode.

Also, make a note of any task that requires resources you do not have, and ensure you keep the resources ready before the date of task execution.

BONUS TRAINING VIDEO — Check my training video on the science behind why we don't do what we want to do- https://www.facebook.com/edlyn.sabrina/videos/10158478047131043/

STEP 7- Schedule your activities:

Once you have created your Master Action-List Worksheet, pull out your calendar or planner and start scheduling the tasks on the list, starting with those with the earliest deadline. Block out weekly time for the specific recurring tasks if possible.

Assess which action steps can be adopted as habits and enter them into the worksheet. People who are living their dreams did not get to where they are with one giant step, but with little steps taken consistently.

STEP 8- Take action:

Even the best laid-out roadmap cannot help you get to your destination without taking action. If you want to change your

"The price of inaction is far greater than the cost of making a mistake."

Meister Eckhart

tomorrow, you need to change your today. Sometimes you are required to take massive action, other times, baby steps. Regardless, execution brings transformation.

STEP 9- Review and revise:

You have your KLSIs, your Success Path, Your Goal Success Plan, and your Master Action-List. Hopefully, you have started taking action on some KLSIs already. Review these worksheets periodically to see if you are on track. You may need to add, revise or remove some goals as you progress. You will be surprised how unexpected opportunities will emerge when you are focused on reaching your KLSIs. Just don't be distracted from your Manifesto and KLSIs, because that will keep you true to who you truly are.

DO IT NOW Take an action step today, however small towards one of your goals.

Conclusion

Congratulations! You have successfully created your personalized roadmap to help turn your KLSIs into reality. A word of caution, do not hold on to it with a closed mind and heart, let it flow. Life sometimes presents some beautiful surprises that you may miss because your eyes are fixated on your roadmap. While you have

QUICK TIP Get an accountability partner who has similar goals to help you stay on track or set reminders to make sure you're accomplishing the required activities to reach your goal.

your eyes on your finish line, release your Success Path and be open to new possibilities.

My Success Metrics My Success Path For My KLSIs

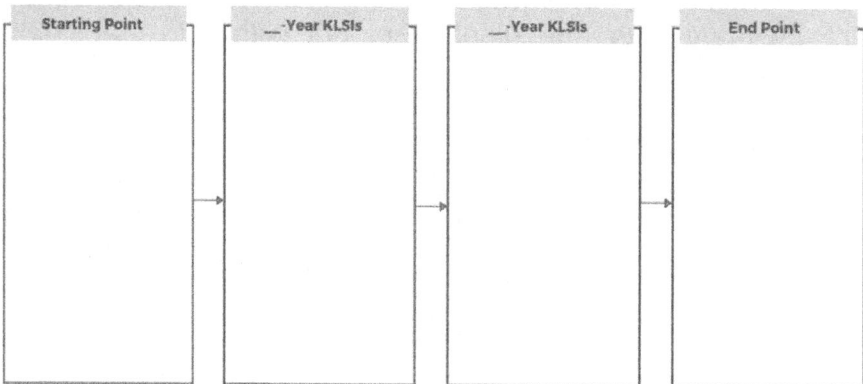

Starting Point	__-Year KLSIs	__-Year KLSIs	End Point

My Success Metrics — My One-Year KLSIs

Mental

Financial

Professional

Relational

Recreational

Spiritual

Physical

Philanthropical

Goal Success Plan For My KLSIs

My Success Metrics

Complete this sheet for each category

Select a Category:
Physical/ Financial/ Relational/ Professional/ Mental/ Recreational/ Spiritual/ Philantrophical

MY TOP GOALS FOR THE YEAR:

1.

2.

3.

MY AFFIRMATIONS

1. I am happy and grateful that I am now...

2.

3.

MY NEW HABITS

1.
2.
3.
4.
5.

My Master Action-List

NO.	ACTION STEP	DEADLINE

NOTES

15

Action Time

We did some deep diving in the past chapters. You now have your Personal Manifesto, your personal Key Life Success Indicators (KLSIs) and a customized roadmap to get there. But even with these valuable tools you have, you cannot get to your destination, without starting the journey. So, it is action time!

The traditional interpretation of action is running, chasing, working harder, working longer, but taking action can mean taking a break, slowing down, working smarter, reframing your mindset, taking time for self-care, reflection, or meditation. Regardless of what action steps you have put down in the My Master Action-List Worksheet in the last chapter based on your Personal KLSIs, action is key!!

When I finally realized I wasn't living a life authentic to me and following my true calling, I had to make some major life-changing decisions to explore my passions, expand my capacity, and start living my purpose of inspiring and empowering others. Your path might not be as extreme, but if your set of KLSIs are misaligned and you don't intend to settle for anything less than what you truly deserve, you will need to take some steps starting today.

> If your set of KLSIs are misaligned and you don't intend to settle for anything less than what you truly deserve, you will need to take some steps starting today.

Take time to go through the exercises in the previous chapters again, if needed, and verify that your new KLSIs are true to you. Discuss them with the significant people in your life who wil be part of your journey. And once you are sure, decide to make changes with resolve, being fully aware that your life is your responsibility.

Research has shown that only 47% of people who suffered from a heart attack made any change to their lifestyle. That shows that we do tend to do things that we know are harmful or can potentially lead to harm to ourselves or those around us. Status quo bias is an emotional bias that involves people preferring that the current state of affairs even when a slight transition can result in massive rewards.

But keep in mind that things will not just fall in place. If your mental or physical health is being compromised, time will not heal you without you taking action. Any pain, strain, crack or tear will only get worse with inaction. Face the reality. If you want something, you need to take a step. Nobody can do it for you.

And what's worse than running away from a problem is deceiving yourself into believing that there is no problem at all. Denial is a common coping mechanism but staying in denial can interfere with your ability to tackle the problem.

> If your mental or physical health is being compromised, time will not heal you without you taking action.

Taking the first step

The first step can be the scariest. You may face fear, self-doubt, and opposition from within and your outer environment. Try to identify what is holding you back and address those areas, instead of going back into your comfort zone. If you think your situation is impossible, remember this:

"Most of the things worth doing in the world had been declared impossible before they were done," Louis D. Brandeis

Don't wait for the perfect day, time or season. if you are waiting to feel ready, you may wait indefinitely. You now have a roadmap created by none other than you to improve your quality of life. If you have any recurring doubts within you, revisit your goals and face the doubts objectively. Refine or revise your goals as needed and take action right away.

Once you have a roadmap, note that you don't need to have total clarity of every street and turn to take. I remember driving in Uganda on streets without headlights. You cannot see the whole road but just a few meters ahead of you and that is enough most times. When you take the first steps, the next will get clearer, and gradually the entire journey will unfold.

Don't let fear of uncertainty, failure, losing control or getting hurt hold you back. Fear is part of us and will always be there to help keep us safe. Feel the fear, embrace it and use the energy to take the next step.

The fear of being judged, criticized or rejected stops many people from reaching out to their authentic dreams. You can either live by others' Success Metrics or you can take action towards creating your version of them; you cannot do both. The naysayers may tear you down, but they are not responsible for your success or failure. Don't let judgment from close people affect your self-esteem and self-efficacy and drive you back to chasing your old KLSIs.

"There are risks and costs to action. But they are far less than the long-range risks of comfortable inaction," John F. Kennedy

If you think people will dislike you or hate you, remember you are not running a popularity contest, and pleasing people is not your goal. This is your life and you only live once. There is nothing more attractive and powerful than a person self-defining their vision and life purpose.

Reaching your KLSIs is a journey. At times, you may need to take a plunge, at other times, baby steps. The end result will definitely be spectacular, but don't forget to embrace the process. Whether it takes one month or ten years, you will live each day with meaning, knowing you are designing your destiny. The journey towards a life you have created is as fulfilling as the destination itself.

> There is nothing more attractive and powerful than a person self-defining their vision and life purpose.

Process of refining

The journey may not be smooth sailing all along, since life entails progressive change and transformation. Diamonds, one of the most valuable stones in the world undergoes a refining process of high temperature and high pressure. In the same way, on your path to

"A diamond doesn't start out polished and shining. It once was nothing special, but with enough pressure and time, becomes spectacular."
Solange Nicole

your higher self, you will require growth and refining.

Failing is normal

Remember failing is normal. Ask anyone successful if they have ever failed. Ask them how they learned their most valuable lessons. Learn

123

to normalize failiure and embrace it as an educational experience and normalize it. And if you fall, pick yourself up, learn your lessons and move on.

I fell on stage, right in the middle of the Mrs. India Uganda 2010 Pageant. I could have decided to stay down and not get back on the stage for the next round. But I chose to go back for another round and was crowned Mrs. India Uganda 2010. The biggest lesson I learned from that fall was, don't wait to be perfect to stand up. Whether limping or still broken, standing up and taking a step will accelerate the recovery.

> The biggest lesson I learned from that fall was, don't wait to be perfect to stand up.

Get the right support

Get support from growth-minded and future-focused people. Many people will give you great standard advice, but they may not understand your KLSIs and your path. For example, if one of your KLSI is to start a business, don't let someone who is still working in his 60s stop you. If you want to reach the top of the corporate ladder, take advice from somebody who has done it and been there. People may mean well but their Success Metrics may not work for you. Those who care and want the best for you will support you, even if they do not totally understand you or agree with you.

Conclusion

If you want fulfillment, meaning, joy, and true abundance in your life, it is up to YOU! Stop making excuses and take action. Build an unstoppable mindset and develop resilience in the face of obstacles as you head towards your personal Key Life Success Indicators. This is not an antiquated Success Path laid by others, but this roadmap is designed by you. Believe in it, own it, keep your eyes on the prize and go!

ACTIVITY

What one action can you take today or this week towards your biggest KLSI?

16

The Tough Decisions

When you notice a misalignment in your current Key Life Success Indicators, the solution may not always be as straightforward as signing up to volunteer, allocating more time for family, or starting a new diet. Some decisions may be life-altering and can impact people who are dependant on you drastically.

Sometimes getting back in alignment with what you were created to be may mean changing careers, quitting a job, or leaving a toxic relationship. I have taken such hard choices and each experience was painstaking. You don't commit to such decisions by just following a hunch or following your heart. I have seen enough people making spur-of-the-moment decisions based on their emotions and living the rest of their lives regretting them. Worse still, you may jump out and land yourself into a similar space.

> Whether the road ahead is clear or not, you need to be objective and put reasonable thought into such decisions.

Whether the road ahead is clear or not, you need to be objective and put reasonable thought into such decisions. This chapter will help you with those hard-to-make decisions.

Take full responsibility for the consequences of your choices.
Ever since my life turned around post-divorce, a few clients unhappy in their marriage, have indirectly 'sought approval' to divorce. But I do not condone divorce as the only solution to an unhappy marriage. I am strongly against divorce, even though I took that path. To me, it was my last option to protect my children and myself, when everything else I tried failed. Regardless of my beliefs, what I tell my clients is that their life is their responsibility.

People ask, "Should I stay?", "Should I leave?","Should I take this path?". However, the most crucial question is "Am I taking responsibility for my life and the choices I am making?". Ask yourself whether you are taking responsibility for the consequences of choosing to stay in a particular space or disconnect from it? Remember, inaction is a choice and indecision is a decision.

Ask yourself whether you are taking responsibility for the consequences of choosing to stay in a particular space or disconnect from it? Remember, inaction is a choice and indecision is a decision.

Ten or twenty years down the line, will you be blaming society, your family, your job, your boss, your children, your culture, or your religion for your life? Will you be able to live your life without regret, regardless of where it takes you? These are deep questions, and they require you to be brutally honest with yourself. This is not about pleasing or impressing others.

By the time I let go of the pretense of a marriage and decided to file for a divorce after being separated for three years, I was very certain about my decision. I had hung on to my marriage for thirteen years. I had done everything I could. I am not saying I was perfect or had no shortcomings. I know that we could have probably worked things out if we sought help together in the early stages of breakdown, but my ex-husband was not supportive of getting counsel. Instead, his approach was that I could leave if I thought we had problems. I tried fighting alone for more than a decade and finally, after stretching myself to a near-breaking point, I decided I had to take responsibility for my life before I snapped. The disfunctional marriage was affecting the children negatively and I realized that I was not protecting the children by staying.

That was one of the toughest and best decisions I have ever made. There were a lot of challenges along the way, my ex-husband after mutually agreeing to divorce, made things very hard for me and continues to do so. It was harder because I was alone with my children in a foreign country, without any family who could come to my rescue. But through all the trials that followed, there has not been a split second when I regretted that decision. Never once have I wished I had stayed. And that confidence comes with the certainty that I had made the right decision.

So, whenever you are faced with a hard decision, the most important question to ask yourself is:
- 5-10 years down the line, regardless of whether things work out or not, is there anything I will regret?

- Am I willing to take responsibility for the way my life will turn out? You cannot blame your friends, your coach, or your family for the consequences of staying or leaving.
- Am I taking responsibility for my action or inaction?

Below are two approaches that I use with clients who are in the midst of making life-changing decisions.

1. Reality Check: Celebrate what Is working, address what is not. In whatever space you are, job, relationships, house, physical location, occupation, or your headspace, accept the reality that you are getting some benefit out of it. That is the reason you have chosen to still be there. I stayed in my marriage for as long as I did for the sake of stability for my kids and to prevent disappointment to my family and church members. The benefits of you staying in a space may be provision, security, perks, status, protection, stability for yourself and the children, etc.

What you need to understand is, it is very unlikely that any space is perfect and gives you 100% what you hoped for. There is no perfect job, marriage, friendship, country, etc. Our unhappiness stems from the unrealistic expectation of perfection, even when we know we are not perfect ourselves.

So, ask yourself, how much are you gaining from remaining in the status-quo in terms of percentage? 10%? 80%? 50%? This is an odd question, but think about a number in terms of your experience in your current space.

> Our unhappiness stems from the unrealistic expectation of perfection, even when we know we are not perfect ourselves.

So, let's say you are gaining 70% from your space. In such cases, there is a tendency to look for that missing 30% outside your space. You may succeed in finding the 30% outside your space but there's a higher probability that you will lose 70% that you are receiving in your current space. This Reality Check thought process can open your eyes to the situation in an objective way. Instead of putting all blame on others, this process can help direct the focus inward, to see if a change within you can improve the situation.

When you are making a hard choice in your career, relationship, diet, house, state, friendship, keep these in mind:

- You cannot get 100% out of any space you are in. Life is not perfect. People are not perfect. You are not perfect. Be grateful for what you are receiving. Celebrate what is working.
- You may quit your space to chase the 30% but end up losing the 70%. You have to decide whether the 30% is worth the loss. Sometimes it is well worth it. But it is for you to evaluate.
- You can play a part in increasing what you get out of the space by increasing what you put in. Have you done all you can? Is there any thing else you can try? Is it worth trying some more?

By the time I left my marriage, I was gaining nothing from the marriage. I was in the negatives. There was uncertainity about what to expect post-divorce. I was not sure what was in store for me outside. But I knew for certain that nothing could be worse than what my children and I were going through within the marriage. Everyone's experience varies and the Reality Check process will help you see your options more clearly.

> **DO IT NOW** Make a list of everything that is working in your favor in your current space, whether relationship, job, etc

2. Cost-Benefit Analysis:

There is a management tool called the Cost-Benefit Analysis that I use in my training to objectively assess a situation and make the right decision. In a nutshell, you assess what you stand to gain and lose, in both cases of taking action or not.

So, if you are in the midst of making a tough choice or if you are facing a dilemma, I want you to ask yourself four questions:

1. What is the cost of taking action? The cost would be anything, tangible or intangible that you pay or spend in the process of taking that step. So, it could be money, time, focus, strain in relationships, loss of status and respect, other resources that you would use, or anything that you stand to lose by taking action.
2. What are you benefiting from taking action? These are things you will gain from taking action. Again, it could be tangible or intangible, e.g. money, promotion, happiness, meaning, etc.
3. What is the cost of not taking action? This is basically what you are losing by maintaining the status quo, e.g., loss of peace, self-worth, confidence, stagnation, ill health, abuse, or potential death.
4. What is the benefit of not taking action?

If two far outweighs four and three is greater than one, then you know it is time to take action. The answers to these four questions will help you evaluate your situation objectively based on what is most important to you.

Many people choose to stay in an unfulfilling job, course or relationship, because what they gain from it (4) is greater than what they will lost if they quit (1)

Cost-Benefit Analysis Example

Decision: To stay or resign from my job (real scenario 2004)

1. What is the benefit of resigning? I would had more time for my children, family and home. I could engage in my passions and purpose. I could explore other opportunities for income.

2. What will I lose? No income for a period, I will have to cut down costs, my savings could run out, my career will be affected, loss of status of an engineer or working woman.

3. What is the benefit of staying? A stable income, status, respect.

4. What was the cost of staying? I was losing myself; the job did not allow me to utilize my potential, I had less time with my family, especially my new baby, the feeling of inadequacy, no job satisfaction.

To me, the benefits of resigning were greater than those of staying and what I was losing by staying in the job was greater than what I would potentially lose by resigning. So, I decided to resign and never regretted that decision. Every person's assessment will vary.

An example of the Cost Benefit Analysis is below:

Note: Different people may have a different takes on the same situation. What works for one may not work for another. What makes one's heart sing, may be unacceptable to another. There is no right or wrong unless there are cases of persistent abuse and infidelity. You make your choice and take responsibility for it.

Choose your battle

Finally, the biggest question, is your battle worth fighting for?

The 'Never say never' and 'Fight or die trying' mindset is great when you are pursuing dreams that are true to you. You can be, do and have anything you want in life, with the right attitude, strategy and resources.

If you realize you are on the wrong ladder and still keep going, then the concept of 'Do or die' may be destructive.

Your persistence and sacrifice will take you high up the ladder, but if you realize you are on the wrong ladder and still keep going, then

129

the concept of 'Do or die' may be destructive. The energy, focus and sacrifices you make in your fight are only worth it if you are pursuing something of a higher value. When the prize of winning is less

When the prize of winning is less favorable than what you stand to lose, then you may win the battle and lose the war.

favorable than what you stand to lose, then you may win the battle and lose the war. In such cases it is ok to quit and come down the ladder. Quitting is not always failing. Such quitting has nothing to do with a lack of determination, persistence, or resilience, but everything to do with the wisdom and courage to choose your battle.

The lie that I was doing the right thing

I gave my whole self to my first marriage. Despite all the differences, I fought on like a good God-fearing wife, through pain, sickness, loss of a child, loss of identity, lonliness, lack of love and care. I never thought of quitting as I believed quitting was for losers. I thought I was doing a great job of persistence, bravery, and resilience. I believed it was better to suffer and die daily in silence and anguish than to go for a divorce. But when I started degenerating, I realized that as much as marriage was worth fighting for, it was not worth dying for. I had to choose to let go. For years I felt I was a failure. But quitting did not make me a failure. Quitting saved my life and allowed my children to get out of a dysfunctional space. I found myself and started thriving again once I made that decision. I am now remarried to the most amazing husband who treats me like royalty every day. I had, at one point, convinced myself that real love only existed in fiction, but because of quitting, I opened the door to an opportunity to experience love in my life.

Conclusion:

Not all of life's questions have simple black and white answers. Sometimes it is hard to make the right choice. The Reality Check and the Cost-Benefit Analysis tools can support you in making well-rounded decisions. Being clear on what you want, what is most important to you, and what you gain and lose by your choices, help you understand your situation better. Sometimes losing a few battles may help you in winning the final war.

Having your Manifesto as your reference point will help you lay out the playing field in a way that is authentic to you because each person may have a different view of the same situation.

17

Conclusion

Congratulations!!!
You have your Manifesto, your KSLs and created your Success Path. Hopefully you have taken some steps towards your Success Metrics by now!! Be patient, enjoy the journey, release your intentions to God, the Universe, or the Cosmic Force, whatever you would like to call Him, while you keep moving.

"Step into your truest power, own your highest talents and create results that are nothing less than monumental." Robin Sharma

Life is like a puzzle. Your set of Key Life Success Indicators is like the reference picture used to put the puzzle together. And the beauty of life is that your life will have pieces from other's puzzles, and you will be part of someone else's puzzle too. It is like one giant magnificent puzzle that you are working out.

As a family, we love putting together puzzles and almost every time we start on a puzzle, at least one of us is convinced that there is a piece missing. Sometimes we look through the whole pile of pieces for that particular piece in vain, but the 'missing' piece, eventually turns up. There are many times in life that you do not see exactly where the missing piece is, and you put your focus and energy on searching for it. Don't let the gaps in your life hold you back, the missing pieces will emerge at the right time, and eventually, everything will fall into place.

> Don't let the gaps in your life hold you back, the missing pieces will emerge at the right time, and eventually, everything will fall into place.

Another thing about putting together a puzzle is that you find pieces that don't seem to belong anywhere on the reference picture. You may be wondering how some parts of your life fit in your KLSIs right now - some experiences you've had, some people you have met or some of the gifts and talents that you have. But as you walk on your true Success Path and see life unfolding you will be marveled at how these pieces fit.

If you think of your past life events, you will see that life is not linear, it does not progress logically, one completed stage after the other.

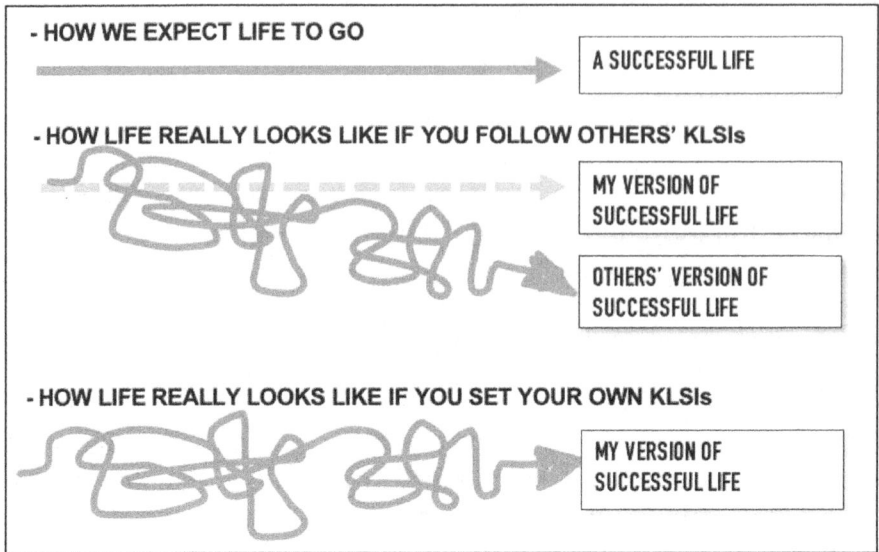

- HOW WE EXPECT LIFE TO GO

A SUCCESSFUL LIFE

- HOW LIFE REALLY LOOKS LIKE IF YOU FOLLOW OTHERS' KLSIs

MY VERSION OF SUCCESSFUL LIFE

OTHERS' VERSION OF SUCCESSFUL LIFE

- HOW LIFE REALLY LOOKS LIKE IF YOU SET YOUR OWN KLSIs

MY VERSION OF SUCCESSFUL LIFE

Being aware of your ultimate KLSIs is the first step toward owning your future. Keep referring to your Manifesto and your KLSIs so you can stay focused on your path. The journey on a Success Path designed by you and not handed to you, is a joyful and satisfying one.

The shift from pursuing others' KLSIs to your own and doing what you were born to do is transformational. Living your life in alignment with your true self, your values, your purpose, and what you really want, will get you excited to wake up and find wonder in each new day. As you step into the greatness that you were put on earth for, you will be able to experience true joy, fulfillment, and abundance in your life.

I wish you the very best as you embark on this journey.

My KLSIs SECTION IV

My Success Metrics My Personal Manifesto

I am _____
_____
_____
_____
_____

I believe_____
_____
_____
_____

My core values are :
_____
_____
_____

My life purpose is to
_____
_____
_____
_____
_____
_____
_____
_____
_____

I declare/commit to_____
_____
_____
_____
_____
_____
_____
_____
_____
_____
_____

Quote

I want to_____
_____
_____
_____
_____

Quote

🔵 My Wheel of Life

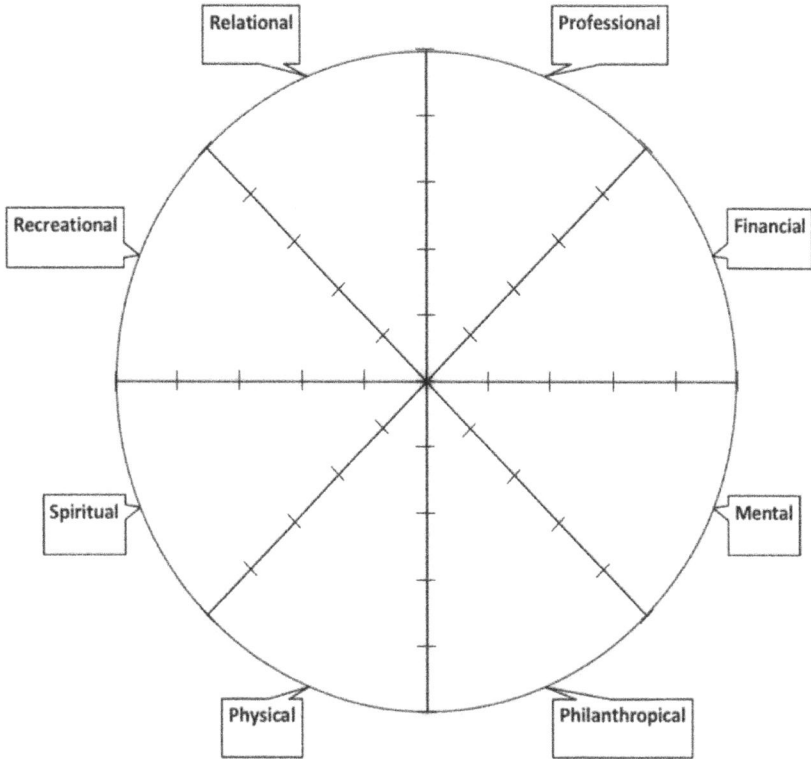

Professional: Job, Business,
Financial: Income, Profit, Cash Flow, Investments
Mental: Learning, Intellectual Growth, EQ, Mindset
Relational: Marriage, Family, Partners, True Friendships
Physical: Fitness, Nutrition, Diet, Self-care
Recreational: Vacations, Hobbies, Recreation, Sports
Spiritual: Purpose, Faith, Ethics, Morals
Philantrophical: Volunteering, Legacy, Acts of Kindness

About The Author

Edlyn was born and raised in India, then lived in Kampala, Uganda for about twenty years, and now lives in Ohio, US. Living in different continents among diverse cultures has helped her see life through different lenses.

As an Inspirational Keynote Speaker and Certified Master Mindset Coach, Edlyn is devoted to inspiring and empowering people, through her talks, writings, workshops, and programs, to live the best version of themselves in line with their life purpose and contribution to the world,

Edlyn loves helping people to ascend from unfulfilling, abusive, or mediocre state of living to a life of abundance, not just in terms of money and fame but an overall, fulfilling, meaningful, and intentional life. She has been working with people from all walks of life to reinvent themselves, starting with reprogramming the way they see themselves and their world around them.

She broke free from an unfulfilling career in Engineering and a dysfunctional marriage and is now living the life of her dreams with her wonderful, supportive husband, nurturing her family, and following her passions of creating, inspiring, and serving.

As a Jack Canfield Certified Trainer in the Success Principles, she teaches proven systems that will empower you too to move beyond your comfort zone, accomplish massive, unbelievable goals and create and extraordinary life for yourself. She specializes in helping people crush their mental blocks, clarify their dreams and strategically create a roadmap to reach them.

Other Services Offered by Edlyn

DOWNLOAD WORKSHEETS You can access printable versions of the worksheets and other tools used in the exercises here: https://www.edlynsabrina.com/successmetricstoolkit

JOIN THE FB GROUP To be part of a community of like-minded people who have made a decision to redefine their Success Metrics and rewrite their story, join the FB Group, Redefine Your Success Metrics. This group is strictly for the readers to share your progress and support, encourage and cheer each other on this journey.
https://www.facebook.com/groups/successmetrics

CHECK BLOG Check out Edlyn's blogs for more inspiration woven around her experiences around the world.
https://www.edlynsabrina.com/blog

THE GAME CHANGER'S LAUNCHPAD If you or someone you know needs inspiration, empowerment and a supportive community to up-level your game and create the results you desire, join my free FB Group,
https://www.facebook.com/groups/thegamechangerslaunchpad

REDEFINE YOUR SUCCESS METRICS PROGRAM Edlyn has introduced a "Redefine your Success Metrics" Program to help you make the most of this book. In this program, you will receive direct help from her on your journey. It includes videos trainings, a workbook, live Q&A sessions, and 6 online coaching calls where you can get help with your own Key Life Success. For more info:
https://www.edlynsabrina.com/redefineyoursuccessmetrics

BOOK EDLYN If you want to book Edlyn to talk to your team or group, connect with her herc:
www.edlynsabrina.com

Connect with me on LinkedIn:
www.linkedin.com/in/edlyn-sabrina

One More Thing
Before You Go

If you enjoyed reading this book or found it useful, I'd be very grateful if you'd post a short review on Amazon. Your support really does make a difference. Also, I read all the reviews personally, so I can get your feedback and make this book even better.

If you would like to leave a review, then all you need to do is click the review link on Amazon here:
https://amzn.to/34nzIzq

 And if you live in the UK, you can leave it here:
https://amzn.to/3vxtCIQ

Thanks again for your support!

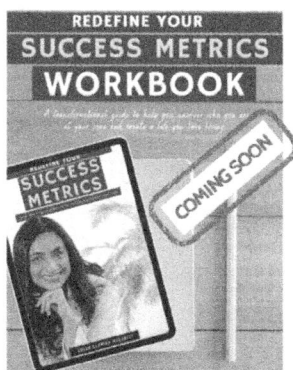

Made in the USA
Monee, IL
09 November 2021